NEWMAN SPRINGS PUBLISHING
320 Broad Street
Red Bank, NJ 07701

First originally published by Newman Springs Publishing 2022

Cover and photography by Cindy McDaniel
eyefordigitalart.com
Paintings by Greg Catmell
Gregcartmell.com

ISBN 978-1-68498-195-3 (Hardcover)
ISBN 978-1-68498-196-0 (Digital)

Printed in the United States of America

Beyond Southern

RECIPES FROM THE HEART

DEBORAH MARTIN

*One cannot think well, love well, sleep
well, if one has not dined well.*
—Virginia Woolf

INTRODUCTION

Welcome to *Beyond Southern*, recipes from the heart by a girl with a passion for cooking Southern cuisine. Inspired by the Food Network, I was chosen to appear on their *Ultimate Recipe Showdown—Hometown Favorites*. Family, friends, and even strangers asked *when* a cookbook was going to be written. After much thought and many tastings by friends and family, this book began.

The first pages stem for the love of cooking with three generations in the kitchen. I remember the loving hands of Granny and the simple wedding band she wore that prepared a modest yet scrumptious meal. Fresh vegetables from the garden out back, and cornbread always broken, never cut. She said, "The Lord broke bread and so shall we." This soft-spoken woman worked hard and loved like no other.

Mother cooked like Granny but admitted she was not the better cook; nothing could compare to Granny's home cooking.

The kitchen's aroma of steaming hot biscuits, rolled by hand, and the thin light brown gravy called us for breakfast. Daddy would crumble a biscuit on my plate and pour gravy over the pieces. I would always tell him, "Reround, Daddy, reround!" Every morsel had to be smothered and covered. I still can see Mother's biscuits warmly nestled together, so light and fluffy.

One of my fondest childhood memories was sitting at the kitchen table for our family meals. Summers would bring fresh vine-ripe tomatoes, sliced with a sprinkle of sugar and crispy fried okra (oak-ree).

Sometimes, we would go swimming at the creek, and Daddy would put a watermelon in the cool creek water. Diving into a slice of sweet, cold watermelon, juice running down your arms—now that is summer in the South.

Beyond Southern does not require expertise to make the dish successful. For most, the starting point is Southern ingredients. However, Southern doesn't come from any one thing, but a myriad of traditions, techniques, ingredients, and flavors. I am nostalgic for the style of Southern cooking, a comforting gift we give to our family and friends. It is not about the food being gourmet, but being delicious and putting a smile on someone's face. In fact, some of my favorite recipes are simple dishes.

Along with recipes from my personal collection, *Beyond Southern* is peppered with dishes graciously shared by family and friends. I have cooked every recipe in this book and hundreds more over the years. Delicious food is an essential of life, and hours spent in the kitchen is time well spent. After all, cooking is a form of meditation that transcends one into a world that reaches all of the five senses.

The best advice I can give you is to read the recipe before you begin. Read it again, and then get all the ingredients together.

Build a repertoire of dishes you enjoy cooking for family, friends, and parties. Memorize them, then make them your own by adding other ingredients or taking ingredients away. Take chances; add your own twists. All recipes are based on generations of cooks' and chefs' ideas. We build on each other's work. After all, a recipe has no soul. You, as the cook, must bring soul to the recipe.

I hope *Beyond Southern* gives you passion for what you create and that you enjoy the culinary journey in these pages.

Boun appetite!

If you go back far enough in cookery, you realize that you are not an inventor, only a re-creator.

—Michael Guerrad

CONTENTS

Simple Beginnings

APPETIZERS, HORS D'OEUVRES, SNACKS

Hors d'oeuvre: A ham sandwich cut into forty pieces.
—JACK BENNY

CRANBERRY CHEESE BALL

INGREDIENTS

4 oz. cream cheese, room temperature
4 oz. goat cheese, room temperature
3/4 cup minced dried cranberries
Salt and pepper to taste
3/4 cup pecans, toasted and chopped

DIRECTIONS

1) Mix cream cheese and goat cheese until thoroughly combined and smooth.
2) Add cranberries, salt, and pepper and mix until thoroughly combined.
3) With a teaspoon, form mixture into balls.
4) Roll each ball in toasted and chopped pecans.
5) Chill until ready to serve.

➢ You can make one big cheese ball and serve with crackers.
➢ Add the pecans to the cheese mixture and roll in the cranberries.

SAUSAGE AND HERB BALLS

INGREDIENTS

3 cups Bisquick
1 pound hot sausage, cooked and drained
1 pound extra sharp cheddar cheese, grated and melted
1 teaspoon fresh rosemary, finely chopped
1 teaspoon fresh flat-leaf parsley, finely chopped

Preheat oven to 350°F.

DIRECTIONS

1) Combine Bisquick, cooked and drained sausage, and melted cheese.
2) Stir in rosemary and parsley.
   * *Shape into balls the size of a quarter*
3) Bake them for 20 minutes or until browned.

Yield: 5 to 6 dozen

Note: In place of Bisquick, you can use the following:

3 cups all-purpose flour
1 1/2 teaspoons baking powder
3/4 teaspoon kosher salt
3/4 teaspoon fresh ground black pepper
1/4 teaspoon ground red pepper

Mix all ingredients together. Proceed with step 1.

Note: Always use freshly grated cheese. Preshredded cheese is coated with cellulose to prevent clumping, which can be helpful but lacks the flavor and creaminess of the freshly grated. It also fails to melt properly and tends to dry out faster.

BACON AND TOMATO GUACAMOLE

INGREDIENTS

5 slices medium-thick bacon, finely chopped and fried crisp
3 large avocados, halved, seeded, and peeled
1/2 medium red onion, chopped 1/4-inch pieces
2 to 3 canned chipotle chilies, stemmed, seeds removed and finely chopped
1 large tomato, cored, seeded, and chopped 1/4-inch pieces
1/4-cup coarsely chopped fresh cilantro
1/4-teaspoon kosher salt
2 tablespoons fresh lime juice

DIRECTIONS

1) Coarsely mash avocados with a fork.
2) Put all ingredients in a large bowl.
   * Toss gently to combine.
3) Cover and refrigerate until ready to serve.

*Serve with tortilla chips!

With a love of gazpacho, bloody Mary, and crab, I thought why not combine variations of the three for a unique appetizer or hors d'oeuvre.

CRAB SHOOTERS

INGREDIENTS

2 cups clamato juice
1/2 cup tomato juice
1/2 red bell pepper, finely chopped
1/2 orange or yellow bell pepper, finely chopped
1 jalapeno pepper, finely chopped
1/2 to 1 avocado, finely chopped
1/4 cup cilantro, chopped (can substitute with flat leaf parsley, Italian)
1 clove garlic, minced
2 tablespoons fresh lime juice
2 tablespoons apple cider vinegar
1/4 to 1 tablespoon Tabasco (according to your heat preference)
1 1/2 teaspoon kosher salt
1 teaspoon freshly ground black pepper
1 teaspoon ground cumin
8 ounces jumbo lump crab, cartilage and shells removed
1/2 English cucumber, finely diced

DIRECTIONS

1) Mix clamato and tomato juice
2) Add peppers, cilantro, garlic, lime juice, vinegar, Tabasco, salt, pepper, and cumin, stirring gently to combine.
3) Stir in avocado.
4) Chill for at least 30 minutes.
5) Place pieces of crab in bottom of shooter glass or any small glass.
6) Pour liquid mixture over crab.
7) Garnish with chopped cucumber on top.

TRIPLE FLAVOR TORTA

INGREDIENTS

4 (8-ounce) packages cream cheese, softened
1/2 cup grated Parmesan cheese
3/4 cup crumbled feta cheese
1 clove garlic, minced
1 cup frozen spinach, thawed and drained completely
1 cup chopped marinated artichoke hearts
1 cup chopped sun-dried tomatoes in oil, drained
1 cup toasted pine nuts
1/3 cup pesto, preferably homemade

DIRECTIONS

1) Combine cream cheese, Parmesan cheese, feta cheese, and garlic.
2) Beat at medium speed until well combined.
3) Divide cheese mixture into thirds.
4) Combine 1/3 cheese mixture with spinach; set aside.
5) Combine 1/3 cheese mixture with artichoke hearts; set aside.
6) Combine remaining cheese mixture with sun-dried tomatoes; set aside.
7) Line a round 8-inch cake pan with plastic wrap.
8) Spread artichoke-cheese mixture in bottom of pan.
9) Layer half of sun-dried tomatoes on mixture.
10) Spread spinach-cheese mixture on top of tomato layer.
11) Layer remaining half of tomatoes on top of spinach-cheese mixture.
12) Top with remaining cheese mixture.
13) Cover and refrigerate for 1 hour.
14) Invert onto serving dish and remove from pan.
15) Carefully remove plastic wrap.
16) Cover sides of torta with pine nuts.

17) Spread pesto on top of torta.
18) Cover and refrigerate until ready to serve.

*Serve with assorted crackers.

Yield: 1 (8-inch) torta

Southern through and through are cheese straws, wafers, crackers—anything made with cheese and flour. They are served on all occasions. Every Southern woman has them on hand in the freezer for that unexpected visitor.

ROSEMARY CHEESE CRACKERS

INGREDIENTS
2 cups grated sharp cheddar cheese, room temperature
1 1/2 cups all-purpose flour
1 teaspoon crushed red pepper flakes
1/2 teaspoon table salt
1/8 teaspoon paprika
1 teaspoon sea salt
8 tablespoons unsalted butter, softened
2 teaspoons finely chopped fresh rosemary
1/4 teaspoon ground red pepper
1 large egg yolk
1/2 teaspoon water

Preheat oven to 375°F.
Line 2 large baking sheets with parchment paper.

DIRECTIONS
1) Cream cheese and butter.
2) Mix flour, rosemary, salt, red pepper flakes, and ground red pepper together.
3) Add flour mixture to cheese mixture and combine thoroughly.
4) Form into a 14-inch log that is 1 1/4-inch in diameter.
5) Refrigerate until firm, about 4 hours.
6) Using a thin, sharp knife, slice 1/4-inch thick rounds.
7) Prick center of each cracker with fork tines.
8) Mix together egg yolk, paprika, and water.
9) Brush with egg yolk mixture and sprinkle with sea salt.

10) Place on prepared pans and bake 12 to 15 minutes, rotating pans from front to back and top to bottom halfway through cooking.
11) Cool completely; store in airtight container.

Variations:

Stir together 1/4 cup roasted, salted pumpkin seeds; 1/4 cup roasted sunflower kernels; 2 tablespoons toasted sesame seeds; and 2 tablespoons black sesame seeds. Sprinkle on crackers in lieu of sea salt.

Substitute cheddar cheese with Parmigiano-Reggiano; add 1 tablespoon fresh lemon zest and 2 tablespoons fresh lemon juice.

Note: Letting the grated cheese come to room temperature before combining it with the butter yields a smoother, more homogeneous mixture.

Recipes, such as these with short ingredients list, are completely determined by the quality of the ingredients. The shorter the list, the better the ingredients must be. Choice of butter, extra-virgin olive oil, salt, and cinnamon is crucial to the success of the dish. Use the finest possible.

TOASTED PECANS

Preheat oven to 250°F.

INGREDIENTS
6 cups pecan halves, frozen
1 stick salted butter, melted
1 1/4 teaspoon kosher salt

DIRECTIONS
1) Mix salt with melted butter.
2) Spread pecans on a baking sheet.
3) Pour butter mixture over pecans, stirring to coat.
4) Bake for 1 hour, stirring every 15 minutes.

The world's largest pecan nursery is in Lumberton, Mississippi.

CINNAMON SUGAR PECANS

INGREDIENTS

1 cup granulated sugar
5 tablespoons cream
1/4 teaspoon Vietnamese or Ceylon cinnamon
1/4 teaspoon kosher salt
2 cups pecan halves
1/2 teaspoon vanilla extract

DIRECTIONS

1) Bring first four ingredients to a slow boil.
2) Add pecans and cook until thickened.
3) Stir in vanilla.
4) Pour onto buttered baking sheet and separate pecans with a fork.

SWEET AND SPICY PECANS

INGREDIENTS

2 tablespoons unsalted butter
2 tablespoons light brown sugar
1/2 teaspoon kosher salt
2 cups pecan halves
1/4 teaspoon chili powder
1/4 teaspoon ground cinnamon
1/4 teaspoon ground cumin
1/8 teaspoon ground red pepper
1 tablespoon finely chopped fresh rosemary

DIRECTIONS

1) Melt butter and sugar in a large heavy bottom skillet.
2) Add salt, pecans, chili powder, cinnamon, cumin, and red pepper; cook 5 to 6 minutes.
3) Remove from heat; add rosemary, toss until thoroughly mixed.
4) Separate and let cool.

Note: Nuts and seeds, both shelled and unshelled, keep the best and the longest when stored in the freezer. Unshelled nuts crack more easily when frozen. Nuts and seeds can be used directly from the freezer.

ROSEMARY ROASTED MIXED NUTS

INGREDIENTS

4 cups mixed, salted nuts (without peanuts)
2 tablespoons chopped fresh rosemary
1/2 teaspoon ground red pepper (cayenne)
2 teaspoons dark brown sugar
2 teaspoons kosher salt
1 tablespoon melted butter
*Preheat oven to 375°F.

DIRECTIONS

1) Place nuts on an ungreased sheet pan.
2) Bake for 10 to 15 minutes; check after 8 to 10 minutes as they can easily burn.
3) Combine rosemary, pepper, sugar, salt, and butter in a large bowl.
4) Toss the warm nuts with rosemary mixture until completely coated.
5) May be served warm or at room temperature.

These insanely tasty cocktail nuts—inspired by a recipe from entertaining guru Ina Garten, a.k.a. Barefoot Contessa—are the perfect little something for guests to munch on while you finish cooking.

GOAT CHEESE MINI TARTS

INGREDIENTS

2 packages mini Phyllo shells
2 (4-ounce) logs of goat cheese, room temperature
1(12-ounce) jar apricot preserves
1/2 cup chopped, sweet and spicy walnuts

DIRECTIONS

1) Place 1 teaspoon goat cheese in each mini shell.
2) Top with 1/2 teaspoon apricot preserves.
3) Sprinkle with chopped sweet and spicy pecans.[1]
4) Chill until ready to serve.

Note: The goat cheese and apricot preserves can be mixed together in lieu of
    layering.
Yield: 24

---

[1] Sweet & Spicy Pecans pg. 15.

BLOOMING STRAWBERRIES

INGREDIENTS

8 ounces mascarpone, softened
1/4 cup confectioner's sugar
1/4 teaspoon vanilla extract
2 tablespoons fresh lemon juice
2/3 cup chopped pecans
1 quart fresh strawberries

DIRECTIONS

1) Wash strawberries, remove stems, and drain.
2) Make four cuts into the point of the strawberry, almost down to the stem end.
3) Blend mascarpone, confectioner's sugar, vanilla, and lemon juice until smooth.
4) Add 1/3 cup chopped pecans and mix until combined.
5) Put mixture into a piping bag and pipe into each strawberry.
6) Sprinkle with remaining pecans and refrigerate until ready to serve.

This was my signature dish when I competed on the Food Network's *Ultimate Recipe Showdown—Hometown Favorites*. When I was heating my oil, the thermometer broke spilling mercury into the oil. I had to start over, and my beignets did not have time to cook in the middle; however, I had the best time and I hope to compete again.

CRAWFISH BEIGNETS WITH SPICY REMOULADE

INGREDIENTS

Beignets

2 cups all-purpose flour
2 tablespoons baking powder
1/2 teaspoon ground ginger
1 teaspoon ground red pepper
1/4 teaspoon salt
Zest of one lemon
2 cloves of garlic, minced or chopped fine
1 1/2 cups cooked crawfish tails, chopped
3 tablespoons chopped Italian parsley
3 dashes of Louisiana hot sauce (Tabasco or your favorite)
1 to 1 1/2 cups water or shrimp/seafood stock

Remoulade

2 cups mayonnaise
1/2 cup prepared horseradish, drained
1 to 2 teaspoons kosher salt
1 teaspoon ground red pepper
1/2 cup chopped capers

1/2 cup Creole mustard
1/2 cup fresh lemon juice
1 teaspoon freshly ground black pepper
2 tablespoons chopped Italian parsley
4 green onions, chopped, both green and white part

DIRECTIONS

Beignets

1) Mix dry ingredients.
2) Add lemon zest, garlic, crawfish, parsley, and hot sauce.
3) Mix gently until well blended.
4) Add stock/water slowly until a loose dough is formed.
5) Set aside for 15 minutes.
6) Spoon 1 heaping teaspoon dough into hot oil (325°F to 350°F) and cook in batches until deeply golden brown, about 4 to 5 minutes.
7) Remove from oil and drain on paper towels.
8) Sprinkle with sea salt while still hot.
9) Let temperature of oil return to 325°F to 350°F between batches.

Remoulade

1) Whisk first seven ingredients together until well blended.
2) Stir in parsley, capers, and green onions, mixing well.
3) Refrigerate until ready to use.

*Serves 8 people with 3 beignets each!

BB FRITTERS

INGREDIENTS

3/4 cup all-purpose flour
1/3 cup light brown sugar, packed
1/4 teaspoon salt
1/8 teaspoon baking soda
2 slices bacon, cooked and finely crumbled
1/4 cup milk
1/3 cup very ripe mashed banana
1 egg, lightly beaten
1 teaspoon vanilla
Peanut oil

DIRECTIONS

1) Pour oil 2 inches deep in a Dutch oven; preheat to 325°F.
2) Sift flour, sugar, baking powder, salt, and baking soda together.
3) Stir in bacon.
4) Whisk milk, banana, egg, and vanilla to combine.
5) Fold milk mixture into flour mixture and stir until fully combined.
    * Batter will be thick.
6) Drop by rounded teaspoons or small ice cream scoop into hot oil.
7) Fry, turning once, until golden brown, about 1 1/2 minutes per side.
8) Remove from oil and place on paper towel to drain.

*Serve with Peanut Butter Sauce.[2]

Yield: 24

---

[2] Peanut Butter Sauce pg. 175.

*He chopped up peppers, mixed them with vinegar, and Avery
Island salt, put the mixture in wooden barrels to age and
funneled the resulting sauce into secondhand cologne bottles.*
—James Conaway (On the invention of Tabasco)

ZESTY SHRIMP DIP

INGREDIENTS

2 pounds cooked, peeled and deveined shrimp
1/2 cup mayonnaise
1/4 cup minced fresh green onions
4 teaspoons Tabasco
8 ounces cream cheese, softened
1 tablespoon fresh ground horseradish
1 cup Thousand Island salad dressing
1 small yellow onion, grated
1 tablespoon Lawry's seasoned salt

DIRECTIONS

1) Chop cooked shrimp.
2) Combine cream cheese, mayonnaise, and salad dressing.
3) Stir in shrimp, minced green onion, grated yellow onion, Tabasco, seasoned salt, and horseradish.

*Serve with assorted crackers!

Yield: 1 1/2 quarts

Wild American shrimp have more flavor-building compounds from their varied diet than the imported pond-raised varieties. Not only that, but wild shrimp are meatier because they're literally swimming for their lives. Pond-raised shrimp don't have currents in their waters, so farmers have to add antibodies to keep the shrimp healthy.

PICKLED SHRIMP

INGREDIENTS

5 pounds medium shrimp
1 celery stalk, cut into pieces
4 sprigs flat-leaf parsley
1 onion quartered
1 lemon, quartered
2 cups artichoke hearts, quartered
3/4 cup champagne vinegar
4 bay leaves
1 teaspoon dry mustard
2 medium sweet onions, quartered and very thinly sliced

1 lemon, sliced
1 tablespoon kosher salt
1 red bell pepper, thinly sliced
4 lemons, thinly sliced
1 cup extra-virgin olive oil
1/2 cup white wine vinegar
1/2 cup fresh lemon juice
2 tablespoons small capers, drained
4 teaspoons pickling spice
1/4 to 1/2 teaspoon Louisiana hot sauce

To Cook Shrimp
1) Fill a large pot with water.
2) Add onion, celery, lemon, and parsley.
3) Bring to a boil over high heat; reduce and simmer 15 to 20 minutes.
4) Add the shrimp.
5) As soon as water returns to a simmer, remove from heat.
   * The shrimp will just have begun to curl and have turned a bright pink.
   * Do not allow the water to boil, or the shrimp will be tough.

DIRECTIONS

1) Layer shrimp, onion, artichoke hearts, and lemon slices in a shallow dish that is deep enough to stir ingredients without spilling.
2) Combine canola oil, white wine vinegar, champagne vinegar, and lemon juice, mixing well.
3) Add bay leaves, capers, dry mustard, kosher salt, black pepper, pickling spice, and hot sauce, stirring to combine fully.
4) Pour over shrimp mixture; cover and refrigerate 6 to 24 hours, turning often.
5) A large plastic bag placed in a bowl can be used to marinate ingredients.

Thirst Quenchers

COCKTAILS, PUNCHES, TEAS

Cocktails are society's most enduring invention!
—ELSA MAXWELL

Annie Abraham ran a catering company in Meridian for many years. Two things everyone requested were her Hot Crab Dip and her Punch. I was fortunate enough to get her punch recipe, but I haven't found anyone who has her recipe for Hot Crab Dip.

MISS ANNIE'S PUNCH

INGREDIENTS
2 large cans pineapple juice
2 large cans frozen lemonade, thawed
2 large cans frozen limeade, thawed
Two 2-liter bottles ginger ale or Sprite

DIRECTIONS
1) Mix pineapple juice, lemonade, and limeade.
2) Pour half into gallon ice cream bucket or ice ring.
3) Place in freezer until frozen solid, preferably overnight.
4) Place frozen mix into bottom of punch bowl.
5) Slowly pour remaining mixture over frozen mixture.
6) Pour one bottle of ginger ale or Sprite into punch bowl.
7) When half of the frozen mixture has melted, add remaining bottle of soda.

Iced tea—sometimes so sweet you can barely taste the tea—is a staple beverage of the South. The iced tea of my childhood was made exclusively with Red Diamond tea bags. Mother mixed the hot brew with sugar until it was a nice, thick syrup then added cold water. Southern tea is always served in a glass filled to the brim with ice.

SOUTHERN SWEET TEA

INGREDIENTS

2 cups water
3 family-size tea bags
1 cup granulated sugar
7 cups cold water

DIRECTIONS

1) Bring 2 cups water to a boil in a saucepan.
2) Remove from heat and add tea bags.
3) Cover and steep 10 minutes and then discard tea bags.
4) Add sugar, stirring until dissolved.
5) Pour into a 1 gallon container.
6) Add 7 cups cold water, stir until combined, and serve over ice.

In the movie *Steel Magnolias*, Truvy, played by Dolly Parton, proclaimed, "It is the house wine of the South."

Note: Dissolve old-fashioned lemon drops in your tea for a nice flavor. They melt quickly and keep the tea brisk.

SIMPLE SYRUP

INGREDIENTS
1 cup granulated sugar
1 cup water

DIRECTIONS
1) Combine in medium saucepan over medium heat until sugar dissolves.
2) Increase heat and bring to a boil.
3) Reduce heat and simmer 3 minutes.
4) Remove from heat and let cool.

Note: This syrup is easy to make, and because the sugar is dissolved, it blends easily in teas, lemonade, and cocktails. There are many variations on simple syrup depending upon what beverage you are making.

FRESH LEMONADE

INGREDIENTS

2 cups fresh lemon juice
2 1/2 cups lemonade syrup
4 cups cold water

DIRECTIONS

1) Mix in a pitcher and chill until ready to serve.
2) Pour over ice-filled glasses, and garnish with a lemon twist.

LEMONADE SYRUP

INGREDIENTS

1 1/4 cups water
1 1/4 cups granulated sugar
4 lemon halves (juiced)

DIRECTIONS

1) Combine in a saucepan over medium heat; bring to a boil.
2) Continue stirring until sugar is melted.
3) Remove from heat and let cool.

Note: For a more sophisticated, complex, and exotic taste, add 1/2 vanilla bean split to the sugar water.

*For an extra kick, add a shot of vodka or rum and a splash of soda.

MINT TEA PUNCH

INGREDIENTS

6 cups boiling water
5 tea bags
6 sprigs fresh mint
2 cups granulated sugar
3/4 cup fresh lemon juice
10 ounces pineapple juice
16 ounces ginger ale

DIRECTIONS

1) Pour water over mint and tea.
2) Steep 5 minutes.
3) Remove mint and add sugar, lemon juice, and pineapple juice.
4) Add ginger ale just before serving!

1 1/2 times recipe makes 1 gallon = 25 people

If life gives you lemons, make lemonade.
If life gives you tomatoes, make bloody Marys.

—Unknown

BLOODY MARY

INGREDIENTS

32-ounce bottle tomato juice

8 ounces vodka

4 ounces V8 juice

8 teaspoons Pickapeppa Sauce

1 teaspoon freshly grated horseradish

1/4 teaspoon freshly ground black pepper

1/2 teaspoon of celery salt

4–6 dashes of Tabasco

Kosher salt to taste

Freshly squeezed lemon and/or lime juice

DIRECTIONS

1) Pour all ingredients in a large pitcher and stir until blended.
2) Pour into ice-filled glass.
3) Garnish with pickled okra, cocktail onion, and olive on skewer and celery rib.

*Boiled shrimp can be added as a garnish.

Pickapeppa Sauce comes from Shooters Hill, Jamaica, West Indies. It is made from tomatoes, cane vinegar, mangos, tamarind, raisins, onions, peppers, and spices. Since 1921, the Pickapeppa Company has stuck with their method of aging the sauce in oak barrels for one year. The popular sauce is sometimes called Jamaican ketchup.

Note: I like to pour Pickappepa Sauce over a block of cream cheese and sprinkle with chopped, roasted pecans—makes a great, quick appetizer.

The Latin name for a tomato is lycopersicum—wolf peach. Tomatoes are related to deadly nightshades, which, according to myth, could summon werewolves.

BIRTH OF THE MARGARITA

In 1947, an American couple, Mr. and Mrs. James, was spending the Christmas holiday at their vacation home in Acapulco where they frequently entertained. Mrs. James was particularly fond of a drink favored by the locals: tequila with lime juice. She also enjoyed Cointreau, a liqueur imported from France.

During one very festive evening, she began experimenting with her two favorite drinks and soon poured a concoction mixed from equal parts tequila, Cointreau, and fresh-squeezed lime juice over ice. The Drink, as it came to be known, was the hit of the season.

The following year, the Jameses returned. On Christmas Eve, Mr. James presented his wife with long-stemmed crystal glasses having shallow, flat bowls, perfect for serving The Drink. Etched into each glass was the name of his beloved wife: Margarita. And as they say—"The rest is history!"

CLASSIC MARGARITA ON THE ROCKS

INGREDIENTS
Lime wedge
3/4 cup white tequila
1/2 cup fresh lime juice (about 3 limes)
Margarita salt
1/2 cup powdered sugar
1/4 cup orange liqueur

DIRECTIONS
1) Rub rims of 4 chilled glasses with lime wedge, then dip in salt to coat.
2) Fill glasses with ice.
3) Stir together tequila and next 3 ingredients in a small pitcher, and stir until sugar dissolves.

4) Fill a cocktail shaker half full with ice and add desired amount of margarita mixture.
5) Cover with lid, and shake until thoroughly chilled.
6) Strain into prepared glasses and garnish with a lime or orange slice.

*Serve immediately!

*These are potent yet amazingly smooth tasting when you use good-quality tequila and orange liqueur and thoroughly shake the mixture with ice before pouring over ice cubes to serve.

*After four martinis, my husband turns into a disgusting
beast. And after the fifth, I pass out altogether.*
—Anonymous

LEMON DROP MARTINI

INGREDIENTS

2 cups very cold vodka
1/2 cup freshly squeezed lemon juice
1/2 cup superfine yellow sugar
1 lemon, thinly sliced
Ice

DIRECTIONS

1) Combine the vodka, lemon juice, and sugar in a cocktail shaker full of ice.
2) Pour into martini glasses rimmed with yellow sugar.
   * Garnish with lemon slices.

FROZEN MANGO MARGARITAS

INGREDIENTS

1 (20-oz.) jar refrigerated sliced mangoes
1 (6-oz.) can frozen limeade concentrate, thawed
1/2 cup orange liqueur
Colored decorator sugar crystals
1 cup white tequila

DIRECTIONS

1) Spoon 3 tablespoons of juice from mangoes into a shallow dish.
2) Pour mangoes and remaining juice into a blender.
3) Dip rims of glasses into reserved mango juice, and then dip in sugar crystals to coat.
4) Add limeade concentrate, tequila, and orange liqueur to blender; process until smooth.
5) Reserve half of mixture in a small pitcher.
6) Add ice to remaining mango mixture in blender to 5-cup level.
7) Process until slushy, stopping to scrape down sides.
8) Pour into prepared glasses; repeat procedure with reserved mango mixture.

*Serve immediately.

Serves: 10

Mississippi will vote dry as long as they can stagger to the polls.
—Will Rogers

CINDY'S LAMPSHADE COSMO

INGREDIENTS

1 jigger vodka
1/2 jigger orange flavored liqueur (Cointreau recommended)
3to 4 jiggers cranberry juice
Splash of fresh lime juice

DIRECTIONS

1) Fill a cocktail shaker with ice.
2) Pour all ingredients into cocktail shaker.
   * Shake, baby, shake.
3) Strain into a chilled martini glass rimmed with sugar.
4) Garnish with lime slice.

Note: Cindy is a dear friend that makes the best cosmos in town. When we have our "Girls Night In" parties, she is our go to Cosmo maker. Rumor has it that if you drink too many, you may end up with a lampshade on your head.

DEBORAH MARTIN

Few drinks help beat the heat like the mojito. The fizzy, sweet, tart, and minty taste of the classic Cuban cocktail refreshes you from the very first sip.

STRAWBERRY-LEMON MOJITOS

INGREDIENTS

8 lemon wedges
4 strawberries
3 ounces fresh lemon juice
1 1/2 cups club soda, chilled
24 mint leaves
8 ounces white rum
2 ounces agave nectar

DIRECTIONS

1) Put lemon wedges, mint leaves, and strawberries in a cocktail shaker.
2) Use a wooden muddler or back of a wooden spoon and crush the mint mixture.
   * This procedure releases the mint's essential oils, melding them with the lemon and strawberries.
3) Add ice cubes, rum, lemon juice, and agave nectar.
   * Shake it up, baby, shake it up!
4) Stir in club soda.
5) Strain into crushed ice-filled highball glasses.
6) Garnish with a strawberry and a mint sprig.

Yield: 4 drinks

Note: If you use a molasses-based rum like white Brugal, you will get a smoother cocktail. Whereas, with a sugarcane-based rum like white Barbancourt, you will get a drier cocktail.

By *mint*, I mean spearmint, not peppermint, which is too medicinal. Story of mint: Pluto, god of the underworld and a wood nymph, fell in love. A jealous girlfriend turned her into a plant.

POMEGRANATE SLUSH

INGREDIENTS

2 cups vodka
3 cups cranberry juice (do not use cranberry cocktail juice)
3 1/2 cups pomegranate juice (POM recommended)
2 cups orange juice
Juice of 2 limes
1 cup granulated sugar
1/2 cup water

DIRECTIONS

1) Combine all ingredients stirring until sugar is dissolved.
2) Pour into a large, shallow, freezer-safe container.
3) Cover and place in freezer, stirring every 20 to 30 minutes, until frozen, about 4 to 5 hours.
4) Scrape into glasses, garnish as desired, and serve.

Note: Fill glasses 3/4 full and top with pomegranate juice. Stir until slushy, garnish, and serve. Mixture can be made the day before.

Suggested garnishes: pomegranate lobes, fresh cranberries, mint, lime slice

*A fruit is a vegetable with looks and money. Plus, if you let fruit
rot, it turns into wine; something Brussels sprouts never do.*
— P. J. O'Rourke

BLANCO SANGRIA

INGREDIENTS

1 cup seedless green grapes
1 kiwi, peeled and sliced
1 pound seedless watermelon, scooped into 1-inch balls
1/4 honeydew melon, seeded and cut into 1-inch cubes
1 star fruit, sliced and seeded
1 lime, sliced
1 cup white cranberry juice
1 pink grapefruit, seeded, sliced, and quartered
1 tablespoon superfine sugar
3 ounces orange liqueur
3 ounces brandy
750 ml bottle chilled white fruity wine

DIRECTIONS

1) Mix all fruits in a pitcher.
2) Add the orange liqueur and brandy.
   * Let macerate for 1 hour or more.
3) Stir in wine and white cranberry juice.

**Serve chilled!
**Add more sugar if too tart for your taste.

*A bottle of wine contains more philosophy
than all the books in the world.*
— Louis Pasteur

As you get older, you shouldn't waste time drinking bad wine.
—Julia Child

RED-WINE SANGRIA

INGREDIENTS

1/3 cup superfine sugar, to taste
1/2 cup orange-flavored liqueur
1/4 cup brandy or cognac
1 whole orange, very thinly sliced
1 whole lemon, very thinly sliced
1 whole lime, very thinly sliced
1 whole apple, unpeeled, cored, halved and cut into 1/2-inch thick slices
1 (750 ml) bottle Spanish Rioja or other dry red wine
1 cup freshly squeezed orange juice (about 4 oranges)
1/2 cup freshly squeezed lemon juice (about 3 to 4 oranges)
Orange or yellow sanding sugar, for garnish (*optional*)

DIRECTIONS

1) Mix together the sugar, orange-flavored liqueur, and brandy.
2) Pour the mixture over the fruit slices and macerate (*soak*) for several hours or up to overnight.
3) Add the wine and citrus juices and stir to combine.
4) Taste, if necessary add Simple Syrup[3] to sweeten.
5) Refrigerate overnight.
6) Moisten the rim of each chilled glass and press into the sanding sugar, if desired.
7) Fill each glass with ice, and then attach a fresh orange and lime slice to the rim.
    * Pour the sangria over the ice and serve immediately.

---

[3] Simple Syrup pg. 31.

Variations: Add raspberries, strawberries, fresh cherries (pitted), or peaches when in season.

Yields: 1 1/2 quarts

Note: A pitcher of icy cold Sangria is refreshing and delicious, particularly when served on a sultry day. It is traditionally made with robust red wine, citrus juice, an assortment of fresh fruits, a touch of brandy, and orange liqueur.

Rise and Shine

BREAKFAST, BRUNCH, AND BREADS

Ham and Eggs:
A days' work for a chicken
A lifetime commitment for a pig.

—ANONYMOUS

Good bread is the most fundamentally satisfying of all foods;
and good bread with fresh butter, the greatest of feasts.
—James Beard

ONE-HOUR YEAST ROLLS

INGREDIENTS

2 packages active dry yeast
1/4 cup warm water (105°F to 115°F)
1 1/2 cups buttermilk, room temperature
1/4 cup granulated sugar
1/2 cup shortening, melted
4 1/2 cups all-purpose flour (Gold Medal recommended)
1 teaspoon kitchen salt
1/2 teaspoon baking soda

* Preheat oven to 425°F.

DIRECTIONS

1) Dissolve yeast in water.
2) Add buttermilk, sugar, and shortening; stirring to combine.
3) Add flour, salt, and baking soda mixing well until blended.
4) Cover and let rest for 10 minutes.
5) Pour onto lightly floured surface and form into rolls of desired shape.
6) Cover and let rise until double in size.
7) Bake for 10 minutes or until golden brown.

Yield: about 5 dozen

Note: Gold Medal is bleached flour and is best for yeast breads and rolls. It is consistently milled to have moderate protein level (10%). It provides enough gluten structure for a high rise and a texture that is light and feathery rather than chewy.

GRANNY'S SOUTHERN BISCUITS

INGREDIENTS

2 cups all-purpose flour (White Lily unbleached recommended)
3 teaspoons baking powder
1/4 heaping teaspoon baking soda
3/4 teaspoon kitchen salt
½ cup very cold lard or Crisco
1/4 cup very cold butter, cut into a small dice
1 cup cold buttermilk
Preheat oven to 425°F.

DIRECTIONS

1) Sift flour, baking powder, baking soda, and salt.
2) Using your hands or a fork, blend lard and butter into flour mixture until coarsely blended and crumbly.
3) With a fork, briskly stir in buttermilk, just until thoroughly incorporated.
   * You will have wet, sticky dough.
4) With heavily floured hands, pinch off a piece of the dough, about the size of a small onion.
5) Roll into ball and flatten slightly.
6) Place in iron skillet or baking pan of choice, with sides meeting. (This helps to keep the biscuits from searing on their sides, allowing the flaky layers to expand to their fullest).
7) If a crispier biscuit is desired, place biscuits about 1 inch apart.
8) Bake 15 to 20 minutes until golden brown.

Yield: 6 to 7 large biscuits

Note: You must get a quick thorough incorporation of lard, butter, and buttermilk into flour without activating the gluten in the flour, which happens if you overwork the dough.

A successful fluffy and light biscuit is the result of soft Southern flour; good, fresh, very cold lard; butter; and buttermilk, with minimal handling.

Lard gives a flaky texture and a biscuit so fluffy and airy they almost float off the plate. One bite may well move you to tears—either with memories of your Southern grandmother or with regret for not having had a Southern grandmother.

LEMON BLUEBERRY MUFFINS

INGREDIENTS

2 cups self-rising flour
1 cup granulated sugar
1/4 cup fresh lemon juice
1/2 teaspoon ground cinnamon
2 large eggs, room temperature, lightly beaten
8 ounces sour cream
1/2 cup self-rising flour
1/2 cup unsalted butter, melted
1 1/2 cups fresh blueberries
1 tablespoon fresh lemon zest

Preheat oven to 400°F.

DIRECTIONS

1) Combine 2 cups flour, sugar, and cinnamon in large mixing bowl.
2) Make a well in the center; set aside.
3) Stir together sour cream, melted butter, lemon zest, lemon juice, and eggs.
4) Add to flour mixture and stir just until moistened.
5) Mix remaining 1/2 cup flour with blueberries.
6) Gently fold into batter.
7) Fill greased muffin tins 3/4 full.
8) Bake for 16 to 18 minutes.
9) Cool in tins for 1 minute, then cool on wire rack for 10 minutes.

GLAZE

(optional)

INGREDIENTS
1/2 cup sifted confectioners' sugar
1 1/2 tablespoons fresh lemon juice

DIRECTIONS
(Glaze, optional)
1) Mix until smooth and dip the tops of the cooled muffins.

Note: My favorite way to eat a muffin is to cut it in half vertically, spread both sides with butter and toast until golden brown in a skillet over medium heat. Leftover biscuits split horizontally are also great done like this.

At the core of Southern culture is a culinary tradition of foods cherished not only for the nourishment they provide, but also for what they represent. These foods satisfied the body and comforted the soul are inextricably entwined with memories of home in nearly every Southern psyche. Foods often considered ethnic-black oriented are frequently thought of as soul food. However, during lean times, everyone cooked the same thing—foods that were in season or that they had put up themselves. When Southerners are away from home, they often yearn for some good Southern food and fantasize about a bowl of pot-likker and cornbread, our feathery, light biscuits topped with gravy or a bowl of hot grits!

CREAMY GRITS

INGREDIENTS
2 1/4 cups chicken stock
2 1/2 tablespoons unsalted butter
1/2 cup stone ground grits (Anson Mills recommended)
1 to 2 cups heavy cream, divided
2 teaspoons kosher salt
1/2 teaspoon freshly ground black pepper
1 cup grated Parmigiano-Reggiano cheese

DIRECTIONS
1) Using a thick-bottomed pan over medium heat, bring chicken stock and butter to a boil.
2) Stir in grits and return to a boil.
3) Reduce heat and cook until thick and most of the stock is absorbed, about 15 minutes.
4) Add 1/2 cup cream, reduce heat, and cook slowly for 10 minutes.
5) Add more cream as liquid is absorbed until grits are thick and well bodied.
6) Add salt and pepper; stir in cheese until melted.

*Cooking time will be a minimum of 1 hour!

Note: Grits are a long-standing Southern breakfast staple but has become a chic appetizer or side dish served with various meats and seafood. The "grits belt" seems to stretch from Louisiana through the South to the Carolinas.

BREAKFAST STRUDEL

An egg is always an adventure; the next one may be different.
—Oscar Wilde

INGREDIENTS

1 tablespoon unsalted butter
3 large eggs
1 tablespoon minced fresh chives
1/4 teaspoon kosher salt
1/4 teaspoon fresh ground black pepper
1 can refrigerated French bread
1 pound breakfast sausage, cooked and drained
8 ounces shredded sharp cheddar cheese

Preheat oven to 400°F.

DIRECTIONS

1) Melt butter in a large sauté pan over medium heat.
2) Whisk eggs and chives together.
3) Add egg mixture to butter and scramble until almost cooked through.
   * Season with salt and pepper.
4) Remove from heat and set aside.
5) Unroll French bread on a surface that is lightly dusted with flour.
   * Roll dough to a thin rectangle.
6) Spread sausage evenly over dough, leaving 1/2 inch on all sides.
7) Distribute egg mixture over sausage evenly.
   * Sprinkle with cheese.
8) Starting on one of the longer sides, roll dough in a jellyroll fashion.
9) Rub a little water on the end and press lightly to seal the dough.

10) At this point, the strudel can be wrapped in plastic and chilled overnight.
   * If chilling, add 1 tablespoon orange juice to eggs and chives before cooking.
   * The vitamin C helps eggs preserve their color.
11) Bake for 20 to 30 minutes or until golden brown and cheese is melted.
   * Let cool 5 minutes before slicing and serving.

Note: Use hot breakfast sausage and 1/8 teaspoon ground red pepper to add a little kick. This easy-to-make breakfast is just perfect for weekends or for brunch.

*A bachelor's life is a fine breakfast, a flat
lunch, and a miserable dinner.*
—Francis Bacon

In our kitchen when I was growing up, there was an old jar kept by the stove, which leftover bacon grease was poured. Used in many ways—in cornbread, for greasing pans, for cooking vegetables, and anything that needed extra flavor. If you want a real Southern taste, save your bacon grease. A well-seasoned cast iron skillet is essential for a good Southern-style crisp crusted cornbread. Sprinkle the surface of the skillet with a teaspoon of cornmeal. This crisps the crust and helps prevent sticking.

SOUTHERN CORNBREAD

"The staple that the South depends on most—after bacon."

INGREDIENTS

1 1/2 cups plain white cornmeal
1/2 cup all-purpose flour
1 teaspoon kosher salt
1 teaspoon fresh coarsely ground black pepper
1/2 teaspoon baking powder
1 1/4 cup buttermilk
3/4 cup whole milk
1 large egg, lightly beaten
4 tablespoons unsalted butter, melted and divided
3 tablespoons bacon drippings, divided

Preheat oven to 450°F.

DIRECTIONS

1) Put 1 tablespoon melted butter and 1 tablespoon bacon drippings into a 9- or 10-inch cast-iron skillet; place in preheating oven until very hot.
2) Sift cornmeal, flour, salt, pepper, baking powder, and baking soda.
3) Combine buttermilk and whole milk.

4) Whisk egg into milk mixture.
5) Whisk into cornmeal mixture just until combined.
6) Whisk in remaining 3 tablespoons butter and 2 tablespoons bacon drippings
7) Pour into hot skillet.
8) Bake for 20 to 25 minutes or until golden brown.
9) After baking, immediately turn the cornbread upside-down on a cooling rack.
   * This lets the steam escape, preventing the crust from getting soggy.

The North thinks it knows how to make cornbread, but this is gross superstition. Perhaps no bread in the world is quite as good as Southern cornbread, and perhaps no bread in the world is quite as bad as the Northern imitation of it.

—Mark Twain

MEXICAN CORNBREAD

INGREDIENTS

1 pound ground sirloin
1 medium onion, chopped
2 large eggs, room temperature
1 cup buttermilk
1/3 cup water
1 3/4 cup self-rising white cornmeal
1 (14.75-ounce) can cream-style corn
1/3 cup chopped pickled jalapenos
2 cups shredded sharp cheddar cheese

DIRECTIONS

1) Cook ground sirloin and onion over medium heat until browned.
2) Drain and set aside.
3) Whisk eggs, buttermilk, and water together.
4) Add cornmeal and stir to combine.
5) Add creamed corn and mix thoroughly.
    * Preheat oven to 475°F.
6) Pour half of the cornbread mixture into a hot, greased 10-inch cast-iron skillet.
7) Pour sirloin and onion over the cornbread mixture.
8) Spread jalapenos over the sirloin and onion mixture.
9) Sprinkle the cheese evenly on top of the jalapenos.
10) Pour the remaining cornbread mixture over the cheese.
11) Bake 35 to 40 minutes.

Note: Add a pot of cooked peas or beans and you have a complete meal.

SUN-DRIED TOMATO BREAD

INGREDIENTS

1 clove of garlic, minced
2 tablespoons finely chopped yellow onion
1 package of active dry yeast
1/4 cup warm water
1 cup water, room temperature
1 tablespoon oil from the sun-dried tomatoes
1/2 cup coarsely chopped sun-dried tomatoes packed in oil
3 3/4 cups bread flour
2 teaspoons kitchen salt
1 egg white, beaten

Lightly oil the bowl or container in which you are going to let the dough rise with oil from the sun-dried tomatoes.

DIRECTIONS

1) Lightly sauté the garlic and onion in the oil; cool to room temperature.
2) Stir the yeast into the 1/4 cup warm water in a large mixing bowl and let stand until creamy, about 10 minutes.
3) Stir in 1 cup water and the garlic mixture with the oil; stir in the tomatoes.
4) Mix the flour with the salt and stir into the yeast mixture, 1 cup at a time, mixing well after each addition.
5) On a lightly floured surface, knead the dough until it is soft, velvety, and slightly moist, about 8 to 10 minutes.
6) Place dough in prepared bowl or container, cover and let rise until doubled, about 1 hour.
7) Punch the dough down on a lightly floured surface and knead briefly.
8) Shape dough into a ball and place in prepared container and cover with a towel.
9) Let rise until doubled, about 45 minutes.
   * Preheat oven to 425°F.

10) Make 3 slashes on the top of the loaf; brush the top with the beaten egg white.
11) Bake for 10 minutes, spraying with water 3 times.
12) Reduce heat to 375°F and bake additional 25 to 30 minutes.
   * Cool completely on a wire rack.

Note: Make sure the water for the yeast is between 105°F and 115°F. If it is below 105°F, the yeast will not activate; if it is over 115°F, the yeast will die.

Bowls of Comfort

SOUPS, CHOWDERS, AND GUMBOS

If any one element of French cooking can be called
important, basic, and essential, that element is soup.
—LOUIS DIAT

Black-eyed peas are a traditional Southern good luck dish on New Year's Day. Add a pot of greens (collards, mustard, or turnip greens) for good financial luck. The more you eat, the luckier the coming year will be for you.

SPICY BLACK-EYED PEA SOUP

INGREDIENTS

6 cans black-eyed peas, drained and rinsed
1 tablespoon canola oil
3 cups small diced ham, browned
3 medium jalapeno peppers, finely chopped
1 1/2 cups chopped yellow onion
2 teaspoons kosher salt
2 teaspoons fresh ground black pepper
1 clove of garlic, minced
1 teaspoon garlic powder
5 to 6 cups chicken broth or stock

DIRECTIONS

1) Combine all ingredients in a large saucepan.
2) Bring to a boil over medium-high heat.
3) Reduce to a simmer and cook for 30 to 45 minutes.

Yield: 8 servings

Note: I use ham steak, which I brown and then dice. The ham steak seems to give a smokier flavor.

Stocks are the basics for sauces and soups and important flavoring agents for braises. Although stock making is time-consuming, the extra effort yields great dividends. Always use fresh high-quality ingredients for the best flavor. Freshness is as important in making a stock as it is in preparing a main course.

A good stock is meant to support—not overwhelm—the flavor of a dish's primary ingredient. If you don't have homemade stock, use the best quality canned broth or stock you can buy—low-fat, low-sodium, made with organic ingredients.

BASIC CHICKEN STOCK

INGREDIENTS

4 pounds chicken bones or 4 pounds skinless chicken legs and thighs
2 yellow onions, peeled and quartered
3 carrots cut into thirds
2 stalks celery, cut into thirds
2 leeks, white parts only, washed, trimmed, and coarsely chopped
1 bay leaf
10 sprigs fresh flat-leaf parsley
8 sprigs fresh thyme
1 tablespoon black peppercorns
1 small head garlic, cut in half horizontally
2 teaspoons kosher salt

DIRECTIONS

1) Rinse chicken bones or parts well.
2) Place in 8- to 10-quart pot with just enough hot water to cover.
3) Bring to a boil over medium-high heat and boil for 2 minutes.
4) Drain the chicken and discard the water; return the chicken to the pot.
5) Cover with fresh water and bring to a simmer over medium-high heat.
6) Reduce the heat to medium and gently simmer for 1 hour, skimming the top.

    * Add more hot water if necessary to keep the level consistent.

7) Add the onion, carrot, celery, leeks, bay leaf, parsley, thyme, peppercorn, garlic, and salt; cover with 6 quarts of hot water; bring to a low simmer.

8) Simmer for 2 to 3 hours, skimming the surface of the stock as needed.

9) Strain the stock through cheesecloth or a fine mesh strainer (also called a chinois) to remove any particles of vegetables and herbs.

    * Cool, and refrigerate for up to 5 days or freeze up to 4 months.

Adding fresh herbs after you've cooked the soup will preserve the herbs' fresh, bright flavor.

ROASTED TOMATO BASIL SOUP

INGREDIENTS

3 pounds ripe plum tomatoes cut in half lengthwise
1/4 cup extra-virgin olive oil
1 tablespoon kosher salt
1 1/2 teaspoons fresh ground black pepper
2 tablespoons extra-virgin olive oil
2 tablespoons unsalted butter
1/4 to 1/2 teaspoons crushed red pepper flakes
2 cups chopped yellow onions
4 to 6 cloves garlic, minced
1 (28-ounce) can plum tomatoes
1 quart chicken stock
2 cups fresh basil, chopped
1 teaspoon chopped fresh thyme leaves
Preheat oven to 400°F.

DIRECTIONS

1) Line rimmed baking sheet with aluminum foil.
2) Combine 1/4 cup olive oil, salt, and pepper.
3) Toss tomatoes with olive oil mixture.
4) Spread the tomatoes on the lined baking sheet in a single layer and roast 45 minutes.
5) In a large stockpot over medium heat, add 2 tablespoons olive oil, butter, and crushed red pepper flakes.
6) Once oil is hot, add onions and garlic.
7) Sauté until onions start to turn brown, about 8 to 10 minutes.

8) Add the canned tomatoes with juice and chicken stock; stir to combine.

9) Add the roasted tomatoes with liquid and bring to a boil.

10) Reduce heat and simmer, uncovered for 40 minutes.

11) Add basil and thyme.

12) Pass through a food mill fitted with the coarsest blade or use a hand immersion blender to puree.

**Serve hot or cold.

Yield: 8 servings

RED CURRY CHICKEN SOUP

INGREDIENTS

3 tablespoons extra-virgin olive oil
2 ribs celery, chopped
1 medium yellow onion, chopped
1 carrot, peeled and chopped
2 cloves garlic, minced
3 inch piece of fresh ginger, peeled and minced
2 1/2 to 3 tablespoons red curry paste
4 cups chicken stock (preferably homemade)
2 tablespoons fish sauce
3 cans coconut milk
2 tablespoons cornstarch
4 tablespoons water
1 1/2 to 2 cups shredded cooked chicken
1 cup shitake mushrooms, chopped (*optional*)
1 1/2 limes, juiced

DIRECTIONS

1) Heat olive oil in a stockpot or Dutch oven over medium heat.
2) Add celery, onion, carrot, garlic, and ginger.
   * Sauté until onions turn translucent.
3) Stir in curry paste to coat vegetable mixture.
4) Immediately add chicken stock, fish sauce, and coconut milk and bring to a boil.
5) Make slurry with the cornstarch and water and add to mixture to thicken.
6) Reduce heat and add chicken, mushrooms, and lime juice, simmering for an additional 10 to 15 minutes.
   * Simmer for an additional 10 to 15 minutes.

Note: Thai food delivers unique flavors and some of the most delicious in the world. This soup balances spice from the red curry pastes with the sweetness of the coconut milk. You can adjust the spice level by adding more or less of the red curry paste. To give more of an Asian flair, add 1 to 2 tablespoons creamy peanut butter when you add the liquids. Garnish with roasted chopped peanuts. Garnish: fresh cilantro and lime slices

GUMBO HERITAGE

Debuting in the late eighteenth century, this savory Creole stew is a melting pot of French, Spanish, and African flavors. Its name derives from gumbo (a Bantu word for "okra"), the ingredient traditionally used to thicken the dish. Although every Louisiana cook swears by a signature version, gumbos are united by the use of a rich, dark roux, and nearly all include fresh Gulf Coast shrimp or crayfish. Other than that, almost everything goes.

Indispensable to a good gumbo, okra are slender, ridged green seedpods with pointed ends. During cooking, the cut pods release a slimy substance that thickens the gumbo. Sautéing the okra before adding it to the other ingredients turns it a lovely golden brown and lessens its viscous quality. A dish of file powder (ground sassafras leaves), with a little taste of mild marjoram, also acts as a thickener. Introduced by Choutaus, who lived around Lake Pontchartrain, into Creole cooking, file has become a signature ingredient of the region. Never add file until the end when there is no chance of the gumbo returning to a boil. It is best added only to the portion to be served.

Roux is two ingredients—flour and oil of equal amounts. The slow-cooked blend contributes a rich depth of flavor to Creole and Cajun cooking and is the heart of every true gumbo. Getting the roux to the deep brown, smoky, nutty flavor can't be rushed. Whisking the precious thickener in the oil, at just the right temperature, is a time laboring process. So plan to spend anywhere from 10 minutes to 30 minutes to achieve this perfection. If it has black, burnt specks in it, throw it out and start over.

SEAFOOD AND SAUSAGE GUMBO

INGREDIENT

2 pounds shrimp, peeled and deveined

1 1/2 pounds Andouille sausage, sliced

4 tablespoons canola oil, divided

1 cup of unsalted butter

1 cup all-purpose flour

2 1/2 cups chopped yellow onion

1 green bell pepper, seeded and diced

1 red bell pepper, seeded and diced

2 ribs celery, chopped

3 cloves garlic, minced

2 tablespoons canola oil

1 pound fresh okra, sliced

3 quarts basic seafood stock (preferably homemade)

2 bay leaves

Leaves from 1 sprig of thyme

1/2 cup chopped flat-leaf parsley

1 teaspoon kosher salt

1/2 teaspoon freshly ground black pepper

2 1/2 tablespoons Creole seasoning

1 pound jumbo lump crabmeat, picked over to remove any fragments

1 tablespoon file powder (*optional*)

Cooked white rice for serving

Hot, crusty French bread

Hot red pepper sauce (such as Tabasco or Louisiana)

DIRECTIONS
1) Heat the 2 tablespoons oil in a large sauté pan over medium heat.
2) Add sausage and cook until lightly browned; drain.
3) Wipe out sauté pan, add 2 tablespoons oil, and warm over medium heat.
4) Add the okra and sauté, stirring occasionally until golden brown, about 15 minutes.
5) Transfer to bowl and set aside.

To make the roux:
1) Heat the 1 cup canola oil in a large cast-iron skillet over medium heat.
2) Gradually whisk in flour and cook, whisking constantly, until roux is a dark brown color, about 10 to 15 minutes.
3) Add the onion, peppers, and celery.
4) Cook, stirring occasionally, until soft, about 8 to 10 minutes.
5) Add the garlic and cook for 1 minute.
6) Add the reserved okra.
7) Slowly add the seafood stock, stirring constantly, bring to a boil.
8) Add bay leaves, thyme, parsley, salt, pepper, and Creole seasoning.
9) Reduce heat to medium-low and simmer for 30 minutes.
10) Stir in sausage, shrimp, and crabmeat.
11) Cook until sausage is heated through and shrimp are pink, about 3 to 5 minutes.
12) Sprinkle in filé powder, if desired, and stir for 30 seconds to incorporate fully.
13) Remove bay leaves.
14) Spoon rice into bowls and ladle gumbo over the rice.

*Serve hot sauce and crusty French bread alongside.

Yield: 8 to 10 servings

CRAB AND SHRIMP CHOWDER

INGREDIENTS

1 pound unpeeled and uncooked medium-sized shrimp
1 pound jumbo lump crabmeat
1 tablespoon extra-virgin olive oil
1 medium yellow onion, diced
3 garlic cloves, minced
2 celery ribs, diced
1/4 all-purpose flour
3 cups chicken stock or broth
1 cup dry white wine
8 ounces clam juice or stock (can substitute with fish stock)
5 medium red potatoes, peeled and diced
1 cup whole yellow kernel corn (canned or frozen)
1 tablespoon Old Bay seasoning
1/2 cup heavy cream
1/2 teaspoon kosher salt
1/2 teaspoon fresh ground black pepper
1/4 teaspoon ground red pepper

DIRECTIONS

1) Peel and devein shrimp; set aside.
2) Drain crabmeat and remove any bits of shell; set aside.
3) Heat olive oil in a Dutch oven over medium-high heat.
4) Add onion, garlic, and celery and sauté until tender, about 8 minutes.
5) Stir in flour and cook, stirring constantly for 1 minute.
6) Stir in chicken stock or broth, wine, clam juice, or stock.
7) Bring to a boil; cover and reduce heat.
8) Simmer, stirring occasionally, for 10 minutes.
9) Add potatoes and cook an additional 15 to 20 minutes or until potatoes are tender.

10) Stir in corn, shrimp, crabmeat, heavy cream, salt, black pepper, and red pepper.
11) Cook over low heat for 5 minutes or just until shrimp turn pink.

A soup so thick you could shake its hand
and stroll with it before dinner.

—Robert Crawford

SQUASHED CRAB BISQUE

INGREDIENTS

1/2 cup unsalted butter
1 medium yellow onion, chopped
2 medium potatoes, peeled and cubed
2carrots, diced
2 pounds yellow summer squash, sliced
5 1/2 cups chicken stock
1/2 teaspoon chopped fresh basil
1 teaspoon ground white pepper
1/2 teaspoon ground red pepper
1 clove garlic, minced
1 cup whipping cream, room temperature
1/2 pound jumbo lump crabmeat, picked and drained
2 shallots, thinly sliced and fried

DIRECTIONS

1) Melt butter in a large saucepan over medium heat.
2) Add onion and sauté until tender.
3) Add potatoes, carrots, squash, chicken stock, basil, peppers, and garlic.
4) Cook until potatoes are tender; remove from heat.
5) Process soup in a food processor in batches until smooth.
6) Return to saucepan; stir in whipping cream and crabmeat.
7) Cook until thoroughly heated; sprinkle with fried shallots.

Yield: 8 servings

MOTHER'S CHILI

In Loving Memory

INGREDIENTS

2 pounds ground chuck
1 1/2 cups yellow onion, chopped
1 tablespoon all-purpose flour
7 tablespoons chili powder
4 cans chili beans, undrained (Bushes recommended)
1/2 teaspoon garlic powder
1 teaspoon kosher salt
1/2 teaspoon freshly ground black pepper

DIRECTIONS

1) In a large saucepan, cook ground chuck and onion over medium heat until browned.
2) Drain excess grease.
3) Stir in flour until well mixed.
4) Add chili powder stirring until meat mixture is well coated.
5) Add chili beans, rinse 2 cans with water, and add to pan.
6) Reduce heat to low.
   * Simmer for 30 minutes.
7) Taste and adjust seasoning.
8) Simmer for an additional 30 minutes.

Wish I had time for just one more bowl of chili.
—Kit Carson's last words

Dressed and Ready

SALADS, SALAD DRESSINGS, AND SANDWICHES

A pessimist is someone who looks at the land of milk
and honey and sees only calories and cholesterol.
—ANONYMOUS

A simple green salad is an absolute must in everyone's recipe repertoire. Always choose the very freshest in-season produce—the combinations are endless! Toss the salad just before serving, and use only enough dressing to coat the greens and vegetables lightly. Be sure to taste the salad for proper seasoning after it has been tossed. For that little extra touch, serve on chilled plates.

GARDEN CLUB SALAD

INGREDIENTS
4 to 5 cups baby spinach and arugula
1 cup cherry tomatoes, halved
3/4 cup roasted fresh corn kernels (2 to 3 ears)
1 avocado, sliced
1/2 cup crumbled goat cheese
1/4 cup pine nuts, toasted

Dressing
3 tablespoons white wine vinegar
1 tablespoon champagne vinegar
2 tablespoons extra-virgin olive oil
1 tablespoon Dijon mustard
1/4 teaspoon kosher salt
1/4 teaspoon fresh ground black pepper

DIRECTIONS
1) In a large bowl, combine vinegars, olive oil, mustard, salt, and pepper.
2) Whisk to blend fully.
3) Top with spinach, arugula, and remaining salad ingredients.
4) Toss well and serve immediately.

Note: It is best to roast the corn in the oven or on the grill with the husks on; let cool and then cut off kernels. Frozen corn can be used and roasted in a skillet or in the oven.

A world without tomatoes is like a string quartet without violins.
　　　　　　　　　　　　　　　　　　　　—Laurie Colwin

NIÇOISE SALAD

INGREDIENTS

2 pounds small potatoes (Yukon Gold recommended)
1 tablespoon kosher salt
1 pound haricot verts, stems removed
1 tablespoon kosher salt
2 pounds ripe tomatoes cut in wedges, about 4 small
1 bunch arugula, washed and dried
1/4 pound large pitted green olives
6 hard-boiled eggs cut in half

DIRECTIONS

1) Put potatoes in a saucepan, cover with water, add 1 tablespoon salt, and bring to a boil.
2) Reduce to simmer and cook 10 to 15 minutes.
3) Drain potatoes in colander and put potatoes back in saucepan.
4) Turn colander upside down over saucepan and cover with a clean kitchen towel.
5) Steam for 10 to 15 minutes until tender yet firm.
   * Once cool, cut into thick slices.
6) Add 1 tablespoon kosher salt to a blanching pot or a steamer.
7) Bring to a boil and add haricot verts.
   * Blanch for 1 1/2 minutes.
8) Remove from water, drain, and plunge into an ice bath.
9) Remove from ice bath and drain well.
10) Arrange arugula on a large flat platter.

11) Place vegetables, olives, and eggs on the arugula.

12) Drizzle with a lemony vinaigrette.

Note: If you would like to make this a hardier salad, you can add sliced roast chicken or any seafood (i.e., shrimp, grilled swordfish, crabmeat, tuna—either fresh, seared, or grilled—or canned).

ORZO SALAD

INGREDIENTS

12 ears fresh corn, shucked and silked
*About 6 cups
1 tablespoon extra-virgin olive oil
1/2 cup extra-virgin olive oil
4 cups cooked orzo
1 1/2 pounds cherry or grape tomatoes, halved
1 cup fresh basil, thinly sliced

Dressing
7 tablespoons extra-virgin olive oil
1/2 cup apple cider vinegar
1 3/4 teaspoons kosher salt
2 1/2 teaspoons freshly ground black pepper
1/8 teaspoon ground red pepper

DIRECTIONS

1) Cut kernels from the corn cobs.
2) Heat 1 tablespoon olive oil over high heat and add corn.
   * Sauté, stirring occasionally, until lightly charred.
3) Transfer to a large bowl and let cool 5 to 8 minutes.
4) Add orzo, tomatoes, and basil.

Dressing
1) Whisk 7 tablespoons olive oil, vinegar, salt, black pepper, and red pepper until thoroughly combined.
2) Pour over orzo mixture and toss.

Yield: 20 servings

Variation:
**Omit Dressing Ingredients from Orzo Salad Recipe
1 to 2 pounds jumbo lump crabmeat

Dressing
6 tablespoons grated lemon zest
1/2 cup fresh lemon juice
6 tablespoons extra-virgin olive oil
6 teaspoons honey
3 teaspoons Dijon Mustard
1 1/2 teaspoons kosher salt
3/4 teaspoon freshly ground black pepper
**Drain and pick crabmeat. Gently toss crabmeat with orzo mixture.

Dressing
1) Combine lemon zest, juice, olive oil, honey, mustard, salt, and pepper.
    * Whisk together until combined.
2) Pour over crab and orzo mixture. Toss gently to combine.

Recipe inspired by Ina Garten

DANDELION SALAD

A simple meal of dandelion greens with fried fatback was one of my granny's favorites and is seriously old-fashioned country food.

Dandelion grows both wild and cultivated with bright green jagged-edged leaves that have a slightly bitter, tangy flavor and can be rather strong on their own; however, their hearty texture and sharp flavor makes a great backdrop for the grease and salty pork. Fatback is the layer of fat that extends the length of the hog's back. It is usually fresh, meaning unsalted, uncured, and unsmoked.

INGREDIENTS

1 large bunch dandelion greens
1 (1/4 to 1/2-inch thick) piece of fatback

DIRECTIONS

1) Place fatback in a cold cast-iron skillet.
2) Heat over medium-low heat and cook, turning occasionally, until crisp, about 10 to 12 minutes; remove from skillet and pour hot grease over dandelion greens.
3) Sprinkle with salt and pepper to taste.
   * Serve immediately.

*A little garlic, judiciously used, won't seriously affect
your social life and will tone up more dull dishes
than any commodity discovered to date.*

—Alexander Wright

FRESH CORN AND AVOCADO SALAD

INGREDIENTS

1 Haas avocado chopped and tossed with juice of 1 lemon
*Should be slightly soft with black or dark skin
1 English cucumber, diced
4 ears of corn, shucked and silked
1 yellow bell pepper, chopped
1 red bell pepper, chopped
1 jalapeno, seeded and chopped
1 tablespoon finely chopped garlic
2 tablespoons fresh cilantro, chopped
4 tomatoes, seeded and chopped
1/4 cup red wine vinegar
Juice and zest of 1 lime
1/2 teaspoon kosher salt
1/4 teaspoon freshly ground black pepper

DIRECTIONS

1) Boil corn until tender, about 9 to 10 minutes.
2) When cool, cut kernels from corn cobs.
3) Combine cucumber, corn, yellow and red bell peppers, jalapeno, cilantro, and tomatoes.
   * Gently toss avocado with corn mixture.
4) Whisk together vinegar, lime juice, lime zest, salt, and pepper.
5) Pour over corn and avocado mixture; toss gently.

ARTICHOKE, ORZO, AND SHRIMP SALAD

INGREDIENTS

3/4 box of orzo (3/4 pounds)
1 teaspoon extra-virgin olive oil
1/2 cup extra-virgin olive oil
1 teaspoon freshly ground pepper
2 tablespoons extra-virgin olive oil
1/2 teaspoon fresh black pepper
*If seeds are small, you do
    not have to remove.
1 medium cucumber, seeded,
    medium dice
8 ounce feta cheese, crumbled

*Reserving 2 tablespoons of marinate
1 tablespoon kosher salt
1/2 cup fresh lemon juice
2 teaspoons kosher salt
2 pounds fresh large shrimp
3/4 teaspoon kosher salt
1/4 cup chopped fresh dill
8-ounce jar marinated arti-
    choke hearts, drained
    and coarsely chopped

Preheat oven to 400°F.

DIRECTIONS

1) Bring 6-quarts of water with salt and olive oil to a boil.
2) Add orzo and simmer about 9 to 11 minutes, stirring constantly until al dente.
   * Do not overcook.
3) Drain.
4) While water is coming to a boil, whisk lemon juice, olive oil, salt and black pepper in a large bowl.
5) Add drained orzo and stir well.
6) Place shrimp in a single layer on a sheet pan; drizzle with olive oil, sprinkle with salt and pepper.
7) Bake for approximately 5 to6 minutes, or until shrimp turn pink and are cooked through.
8) Immediately put in an ice bath to stop cooking.
9) Once cool, peel and devein shrimp.

10) Add shrimp, dill, cucumber, artichoke hearts, and reserved artichoke juice to orzo and toss gently until well combined; sprinkle feta on top and carefully toss.

 * Set aside at room temperature for 1 hour.

11) Salad can be served chilled.

Inspiration for this salad came from Ina Garten.

FRESH TOMATO SALAD

INGREDIENTS

2 to 3 large tomatoes, sliced
1 medium sweet yellow onion, sliced
1 cup Champagne vinegar
1/2 cup granulated sugar
2 1/4 teaspoons kosher salt
1/2 teaspoon fresh ground black pepper

DIRECTIONS

1) Place tomato and onion slices in a plastic or glass container in one layer.
2) Whisk vinegar, sugar, salt, and pepper until sugar begins to dissolve.
3) Pour over tomato and onion slices and refrigerate for at least 1 hour.
4) Turning tomato and onion slices after 30 minutes.
   * Let sit at room temperature for 20 minutes before serving.
5) Arrange tomato and onion slices on a serving platter.

It's difficult to think anything but pleasant thoughts
while eating a homegrown tomato.

—Lewis Grizzard

DEBBIE'S SUMMER SALAD

INGREDIENTS

Dressing
1 bottle red wine vinegar
1 bottle of Zesty Italian salad dressing
*Mix red wine vinegar and Zesty Italian salad dressing until thoroughly combined.

Salad
2 cups cauliflower florets
2 cups broccoli florets
1 cup carrots, bite-size pieces
1 Granny Smith apple, sliced
1 Red Delicious apple, sliced
2 cups grape tomatoes, halved
1 small red onion, thinly sliced (sweet onion can be used), optional
**Mix all ingredients together and set aside.

DIRECTIONS
1) Put all vegetables in a large bowl or Ziploc bag.
2) Put marinate over vegetables.
3) Chill 2 to 4 hours, stirring occasionally.

Cauliflower is cabbage with a college education.
—Mark Twain

One fabled comfort food, fried green tomatoes, at one time was hard to find in a restaurant—preparation requires loving hands. As Idgie noted longingly in the movie *Fried Green Tomatoes*, they are "the thing to be missed," piled high on a plate. Like all Southern comfort foods, they are a sign of love and caring expressed in a tangible and delicious way.

This was my Speed Round recipe when I was on the Food Network's *Ultimate Recipe Showdown: Hometown Favorites*. The judges commented that these were the best fried green tomatoes they had ever eaten.

FRIED GREEN TOMATO AND CRAB SALAD WITH SUMAC VINAIGRETTE

INGREDIENTS

6 large green tomatoes, sliced 1/4 to 3/8-inch thick
1 1/2 teaspoons kosher salt
1 1/2 teaspoons freshly ground black pepper
1/2 cup plain white cornmeal
1/2 cup all-purpose flour
2 teaspoons Creole seasoning (Konriko recommended)
Peanut oil
2 bunches baby arugula
1 1/2 pounds jumbo lump crabmeat

Preheat approximately 2 inches of oil in large cast-iron skillet to 325°F.

DIRECTIONS

1) Sprinkle both sides of tomatoes with salt and pepper.
2) Combine cornmeal, flour, and Creole seasoning.
3) Dredge tomatoes in cornmeal mixture. *Fry until golden brown.
4) Drain on a rack with paper towels underneath and salt immediately.

VINAIGRETTES

Vinaigrettes are a powerful and versatile tool for building flavors. They can be used for finishing a sauce or cutting through the richness of meat.

Traditional ratio for vinaigrette is 3 parts oil to 1 part acid. However, I like things a bit more on the biting side, so I tend to use less oil to acid. The best way to achieve the right level of acidity for you is simply to taste as you're adding the oil and stop or add more to please your palate. Remember, you are not going to be eating the vinaigrette plain, so err at first on the side of too much acidity and then scale up your use of oil accordingly.

Shallot and garlic are first combined with the acid, which immediately neutralizes the sharpness and magnifies their aromatic and sweet effects.

Basic technique is always the same: acid, garlic, shallot, salt (so that the salt melts), and then slowly whisk in the oil.

SUMAC VINAIGRETTE

INGREDIENTS

8 tablespoons champagne vinegar
2 teaspoons ground sumac
1/4 teaspoon kosher salt
1/2 teaspoon freshly ground black pepper
12 tablespoons extra-virgin olive oil

DIRECTIONS

1) Mix vinegar, sumac, salt, and pepper.
2) Add olive oil and whisk until combined. Reserve 4 tablespoons.

To assemble,
1) Toss arugula with Sumac Vinaigrette, reserving 4 tablespoons.
2) Lightly toss crab with the remaining 4 tablespoons of vinaigrette.
3) Divide arugula among 4 plates.
4) Place a tomato slice on the arugula; top with some of the crabmeat.
5) Repeat step 4 until you have used all of the tomatoes and crab.
6) Serve immediately.

Note: Sumac is a Middle Eastern spice, which is sold ground or in its dried berry form; it has a pleasantly fruity taste that compliments everything from fish to meat.

A dressing is not a compote
A dressing is not a custard
It consists of pepper and salt,
Vinegar, oil, and mustard.

—Ogden Nash

BASIC VINAIGRETTE

INGREDIENTS
1/2 cup extra-virgin olive oil
1/3 cup white wine vinegar
1/4 teaspoon kosher salt
1 teaspoon Dijon mustard
1/8 teaspoon fresh ground black pepper

DIRECTIONS
1) Combine all ingredients in a screw-top jar.
2) With top securely on, shake until emulsified.

* Can be refrigerated for 2 weeks.

Yield: 3/4 cup

Note: You get what you pay for when buying vinegars. The French are great at making vinegar.

Remember, great dishes start with great products.

LEMON-GARLIC VINAIGRETTE

INGREDIENTS

1/4 cup fresh lemon juice
3 tablespoons water
2 teaspoons minced garlic
1 tablespoon Cavender's Greek Seasoning
1/2 cup extra-virgin olive oil

DIRECTIONS

1) Put lemon juice, water, garlic, and Greek seasoning in a food processor.
   * Blend.
2) Add olive oil in steady stream with machine running and process until thoroughly emulsified.
   * Store in refrigerator.

Yield: 12 ounces

*Best served at room temperature or slightly chilled!

Recipe courtesy of Chef Willie McGeehee

BLUE CHEESE DRESSING

INGREDIENTS

1/2 cup mayonnaise

1 cup buttermilk

2 tablespoons Italian parsley

1 teaspoon kosher salt

1 teaspoon fresh ground black pepper

1/2 teaspoon ground white pepper

1/4 pound quality blue cheese, crumbled

DIRECTIONS

1) Place mayonnaise, buttermilk, parsley, salt, black pepper, and white pepper in a blender jar.
   * Blend until mixed and smooth.

2) Add blue cheese and blend just until incorporated—you want the dressing to be chunky but not thick. It will thicken more in the refrigerator.

3) Put into container with plastic wrap, making contact with the surface of the dressing (this will prevent a foamy surface during storage), and refrigerate until ready to use.

Note: Using the freshest dairy products available will give the dressing a shelf life of at least one week.

SPICY CAESAR DRESSING

INGREDIENTS

1 tablespoon mayonnaise
1 teaspoon fresh ground black pepper
1 teaspoon pureed canned chipotle peppers
4 drops hot sauce (Tabasco recommended)
5 anchovy fillets
1 cup extra-virgin olive oil
1 teaspoon Dijon mustard
1/4 teaspoon kosher salt
1 teaspoon Worcestershire sauce
1 tablespoon fresh lime juice
8 garlic cloves
2 tablespoons red wine vinegar

DIRECTIONS

1) Put mayonnaise, mustard, black pepper, salt, chipotle pepper pureed, Worcestershire sauce, hot sauce, lime juice, anchovies, and garlic in a food processor.
   * Process until blended.
2) Slowly pour in olive oil.
3) Pour in vinegar and process until thoroughly mixed.
   * If dressing is too thick, add a little water until the desired consistency is obtained.

GOAT CHEESE AND STRAWBERRY GRILLED CHEESE

INGREDIENTS

4 ounces goat cheese, softened
4 1/2 teaspoons red pepper jelly
1 1/2 cups fresh watercress or baby arugula
1/4 teaspoon fresh, coarsely ground black pepper
3/4 cup sliced fresh strawberries
6 slices whole grain bread

DIRECTIONS

1) Mix goat cheese and black pepper together.
   * Spread on 1 side of 3 bread slices.
2) Spread pepper jelly on 1 side of other 3 bread slices.
3) Layer strawberries and watercress or arugula on goat cheese bread slices.
   * Top with remaining bread.
4) Cook sandwiches, goat cheese sides down, in a lightly greased non-stick skillet over medium heat.
   * 2 to 3 minutes on each side or until golden brown.

Yield: 3 servings

SLOPPY JOES

INGREDIENTS

2 1/2 to 3 pounds ground sirloin
1/2 green bell pepper, diced
1/2 red bell pepper, diced
1 small yellow onion, diced
3 cloves garlic, minced
1 cup ketchup
1/4 cup sriracha
1 1/4 cups water
2 tablespoons light brown sugar
1 teaspoon dry mustard
1/4 teaspoon crushed red pepper flakes
2 teaspoons chili powder
1/4 teaspoon kosher salt
1/8 teaspoon freshly ground black pepper
1 tablespoon Worcestershire sauce
4 tablespoons tomato paste

DIRECTIONS

1) Brown ground sirloin over medium-high heat. * Drain fat.
2) Add peppers, onions, and garlic. *Stirring to evenly distribute throughout the browned sirloin.
3) Stir in ketchup, sirrachi, and water.
4) Mix brown sugar, dry mustard, pepper flakes, chili powder, salt, and pepper together.
5) Sprinkle over meat mixture.
6) Add Worcestershire sauce and stir to combine tomato paste.
7) Cover and simmer over medium-low heat for 20 minutes.

Note: These are very spicy with complex flavors. Decrease sirrachi to 1/8 cup, red pepper flakes to 1/8 teaspoon, and chili powder for a less spicy version.

BACON, PEAR AND RASPBERRY GRILLED CHEESE

INGREDIENTS

3 tablespoons seedless raspberry preserves
1/4 thinly sliced red pear
8 slices crisp cooked bacon
4 slices whole grain bread or bread of choice
1 to 2 tablespoons unsalted butter
Preheat skillet or panini press to medium-high

DIRECTIONS

1) Spread 1 1/2 tablespoon raspberry preserves on 2 slices of bread.
2) Layer pear, 4 slices of bacon, and 2 slices of cheese on raspberry preserve bread slices.
3) Top with remaining bread slices.
4) Spread butter on top and bottom of sandwich.
5) Grill for 4 to 6 minutes or until cheese is melted and top is golden brown.

There is a little country cemetery in Enondale, Mississippi, where most of my father's family is buried. Large oak trees and quietness of the country makes this little cemetery the perfect place to "rest in peace."

Every year on the third Saturday of May, we gather at the cemetery to mow grass, pick up trash, refresh flowers—anything that needs to be done so the cemetery looks as though it had a groundskeeper. A homemade table between two trees is what the food is spread on for all to enjoy. I vividly remember that pimento cheese on white bread was front and center. Although I didn't care much about pimento cheese, I would eat my yearly sandwich on that special Saturday in May. This is what is known as Graveyard Working.

GRAVEYARD WORKING PIMENTO CHEESE

A Touchstone of Southern Childhood

INGREDIENTS
1 cup best quality mayonnaise
3 medium red bell peppers, roasted, peeled, seeded, and chopped
1 pound high quality, sharp yellow cheddar cheese, grated

DIRECTIONS
1) Grate cheese on the small-hole side of a hand grater.
2) Add roasted peppers and mayonnaise.
3) Refrigerate in airtight container up to 1 week.
4) Use 1/4 cup pimiento cheese per sandwich.

Note: *Jarred diced pimento may be substituted for the roasted red peppers. For a variation, add 1/2 cup toasted chopped pecans and 1/2 cup chopped jarred sweet-hot jalapeno slices and 1 tablespoon liquid from jarred jalapenos.

The Main Event

MEAT, PASTA, POULTRY, AND SEAFOOD

All cooks, like all great artists, must have
an audience worth cooking for.

—ANDRE SIMON

*Fish is the only food that is considered spoiled
once it smells like what it is.*

—P. J. O'Rourke

CATFISH WITH PECAN SAUCE

INGREDIENTS
6 fillets of catfish
1/4 teaspoon kosher salt
1/4 teaspoon fresh ground black pepper
1 1/2 to 2 cups panko (Japanese breadcrumbs)
1 large egg beaten

DIRECTIONS
1) Sprinkle fillets with salt and pepper.
2) Put beaten egg in a shallow dish and panko in a shallow dish or on a plate.
3) Put fillet in egg and then dredge in panko.
4) Heat oil in a skillet over medium-high heat.
5) Place fillet in hot oil, brown on one side, when fish releases from pan, flip and cook until brown and crisp.

Serve with pecan sauce.[4]

Note: For more information on catfish, visit catfishinstitute.com.

---

[4] Pecan Sauce pg. 173.

TRADITIONAL POT ROAST

> *Classic Recipe for Roast Beef:*
> *1 large roast of beef*
> *1 small roast of beef*
> *Take the 2 roasts and put them in the oven*
> *When the little one burns, the big one is done.*
> —Gracie Allen

INGREDIENTS

3 tablespoons canola or vegetable oil

3- to 4-pound boneless chuck roast, trimmed

1 teaspoon kosher salt

1 teaspoon freshly ground black pepper

1/4 cup all-purpose flour

2 tablespoons tomato paste

1 cup dry red wine

1 cup beef broth

1 tablespoon Worcestershire sauce

1 large onion, cut into wedges

4 carrots, peeled and cut into thirds

6 cloves garlic, sliced

6 sprigs fresh thyme

6 sprigs fresh rosemary

2 bay leaves

DIRECTIONS

1) Heat oil in a large sauté pan over medium-high heat.
2) Sear roast on all sides.
3) Transfer roast to a 4- to 6-quart Dutch oven or slow cooker.
4) Stir flour into sauté pan, and cook for 1 minute.

5) Deglaze pan with wine, cooking until liquid evaporates.

6) Stir in broth and Worcestershire sauce.

7) Bring mixture to a boil.

8) Scrape up any brown bits.

9) Add broth mixture to cover 1/2 to 3/4 of the roast.

10) Add the onion, carrots, garlic, thyme, rosemary, and bay leaves.

11) Cover and cook for 2 to 2 1/2 hours in a 350°F preheated oven.
    * Or 4 to 5 hours on high in a slow cooker.

12) Discard herbs before serving.

In the vegetable world, there is nothing so innocent,
so confiding in its expression, as the small green
face of the freshly-shelled spring pea.
—William Wallace Irwin

CHICKEN POT PIE

INGREDIENTS

5 cups chicken stock

2 chicken bouillon cubes

12 tablespoons unsalted butter

3/4 cup all-purpose flour

1 teaspoon sherry

2 teaspoons kosher salt

1/2 teaspoon fresh ground black pepper

1/4 cup heavy cream

5 cups diced, cooked chicken breast

2 cups medium-diced carrots, blanched for 2 minutes

12 ounces 1/2-inch diced small red potatoes, parboiled for 5 minutes

1 cup fresh green peas, blanched (frozen can be used)

2 celery ribs, sliced 1/8-inch thick (optional)

1 1/2 teaspoons chopped fresh thyme leaves

1/2 cup minced fresh Italian parsley leaves

Preheat oven to 350°F.

DIRECTIONS

1) In a small saucepan, heat the chicken stock and dissolve the chicken bouillon cubes in the stock.

2) In a large saucepan or Dutch oven, melt the butter over medium-low heat.

3) Add the flour and cook over low heat, stirring constantly for 2 minutes.

4) Whisk in the sherry.
5) Slowly add the hot chicken stock to the sauce, whisking until smooth.
6) Simmer over low heat for 1 more minute, stirring until thick.
7) Add salt, pepper, and heavy cream.
8) Add chicken, carrots, potatoes, peas, celery, thyme, and parsley; mix well.
9) Pour the filling into a 4 1/2 quart Dutch oven or casserole dish.
10) Brush the outside edges of the dish with the egg wash, then place dough on top.
    * Trim to 1/2 inch larger than the top of the dish.
11) Crimp the dough to fold over the side, pressing it to make it stick.
12) Brush the dough with the egg wash and make 4 slits in the top.
    * Sprinkle with sea salt and cracked pepper.
13) Place on a baking sheet and bake for 1 hour, or until the top is golden brown and the filling is bubbling hot.
    * See basic piecrust recipe, page 183.

Note: You can make this into 4 individual servings. Divide the filling equally among 4 ovenproof bowls. Divide the dough into quarters, and roll each piece into an 8-inch circle or shape of the bowls. Proceed with the same directions for a single pie.

JAZZY JAMBALAYA

An onion can make people cry, but there has never
been a vegetable invented to make them laugh.

—Will Rogers

INGREDIENTS

1 tablespoon extra-virgin olive oil

1 pound Andouille sausage, sliced

1 ham steak, cubed

1 tablespoon unsalted butter

1 medium yellow onion, diced

1 cup diced celery

1 red bell pepper, cored,
    seeded, and diced

1 green bell pepper, cored,
    seeded, and diced

1 cup fresh seeded and diced tomato

2 garlic cloves, minced

1 jalapeno pepper, seeded
    and finely diced

2 teaspoons chopped fresh oregano

1 teaspoon chopped fresh thyme

2 tablespoons tomato paste

6 cups chicken stock

3 cups long-grain rice, rinsed

3 bay leaves

2 teaspoons kosher salt

1 teaspoon fresh ground black pepper

1/2 teaspoon Creole seasoning
    (Konriko recommended)

6 to 8 dashes Tabasco

1/4 cup fresh squeezed lemon juice

1 pound medium shrimp,
    peeled and deveined

DIRECTIONS

1) Heat the oil in a large Dutch oven or saucepan over medium heat.
2) Add the sausage and sauté until browned, about 8 to 10 minutes.
3) Remove and drain the sausage then set aside.
4) Add the cubed ham and sauté until browned, about 8 to 10 minutes.
* Remove and set aside.
5) Add the butter, onion, celery, and peppers and sauté until the onion is translucent, 8 to 10 minutes.
6) Add the tomato, garlic, jalapeno, oregano, thyme, and tomato paste.
7) Stir and cook until all of the ingredients are well blended.
8) Add the stock and bring to a boil.

9) Stir in the rice and add the sausage, ham, bay leaves, salt, pepper, Creole seasoning, and Tabasco.

   * Return to a boil then reduce to low.
10) Simmer, covered for 20 to 30 minutes, until rice is soft.
11) Add the lemon juice and shrimp and stir well.
12) Cover and simmer an additional 2 to 3 minutes.
13) Remove from heat and allow it to steam for 15 minutes before serving.

   * Sprinkle with chopped fresh parsley, if desired!

Recipe inspired by Ina Garten.

Canned tomatoes are rarely a substitute for fresh, vine-ripened tomatoes, but they work very well in this recipe. I use imported San Marzano tomatoes (the finest canned tomatoes available).

LASAGNA

INGREDIENTS

1/2 cup extra-virgin olive oil

1 medium yellow onion, finely diced

4 cloves garlic, minced

1 teaspoon kosher salt

2 pounds ground sirloin

2 pounds hot Italian sausage, removed from casing

1 teaspoon kosher salt

1 (28-ounce) can San Marzano tomatoes, do not drain

1 pound dried lasagna noodles

1 pound Mozzarella cheese, grated

1/2 teaspoon kosher salt

1/2 cup dry white wine

2 bay leaves

2 pounds whole milk ricotta cheese

1/4 cup chopped fresh Italian parsley

1/4 cup chopped fresh basil leaves

1/4 cup chopped fresh oregano leaves

1/8 teaspoon kosher salt

2 large eggs, beaten

1 teaspoon freshly ground black pepper

1 cup grated Parmigiano-Reggiano, divided

DIRECTIONS

1) In a large Dutch oven or heavy pot, heat the olive oil over medium heat.
2) Add the onion, garlic, and salt, and sweat until onion is translucent, about 2 minutes.
3) Add the ground sirloin, sausage, and salt.
4) Cook until the meat is browned, about 10 minutes.
5) Stir in the white wine, tomatoes with juice, and the bay leaves.
6) Scrape the bottom of the pot with a wooden spoon, making sure to get all of the browned bits into the sauce.

7) Season the sauce with the salt and pepper; simmer for 2 hours over medium-low heat, stirring occasionally to keep from burning on the bottom.
8) Remove the bay leaves.
9) Bring a large pot of water to boil over medium heat.
10) Add 1 tablespoon kosher salt and allow water to return to a boil.
11) Add the noodles and cook until al dente.
    * Do not overcook as noodles will continue to cook in the oven.
12) Drain well and set aside.
13) Mix together the ricotta, parsley, basil, oregano, salt, eggs, and 1/2 cup Parmigiano-Reggiano.
    * Preheat oven to 350°F.
14) Grease heavily a lasagna pan or large roasting pan.
15) Spread 1 cup of sauce on the bottom of prepared pan.
16) Arrange a layer of noodles followed by a layer of sauce.
17) And then some of the ricotta mixture.
18) Smoothing it with a spatula to the edges, sprinkle on a layer of mozzarella.
19) Repeat the process until the pan is full.
20) Finish with a final layer of noodles, sauce, mozzarella, and remaining Parmigiano-Reggiano.
21) Cover with foil and bake for 1 hour.
22) Uncover and bake an additional 30 minutes.
    * Let rest for 5 to10 minutes before serving.

Note: Al dente is an Italian term meaning "to the tooth" and is used in reference to the degree of doneness of pasta, risotto, or vegetables. The food should be cooked only until it is still slightly chewy when biting into it. It should not be soft and overdone nor have a hard center.

ITALIAN MEATBALLS

INGREDIENTS

1 pound ground pork

1 1/2 pounds ground chuck

1 cup fresh breadcrumbs soaked in 1/4 cup whole milk

1/2 cup chopped fresh Italian parsley

1 cup ground Parmigiano-Reggiano cheese

1 teaspoon kosher salt

1/2 teaspoon fresh ground black pepper

1 teaspoon minced garlic

1 1/2 teaspoons minced shallots

2 tablespoons extra-virgin olive oil

DIRECTIONS

1) Place pork and chuck in a large bowl.
2) Add soaked breadcrumbs, parsley, cheese, salt, pepper, garlic, and shallots to meat.
    * Mix to combine thoroughly.
3) Using about 1/4 cup of mixture, shape into 1 1/2-inch balls.
4) Line a baking sheet with non-stick aluminum foil and set aside.
5) Preheat oven to 350°F.
6) In a large fry pan, warm olive oil over medium heat.
7) Brown meatballs in batches, on all sides.
8) Place browned meatballs on prepared pan.
9) Bake for 15 minutes.
    * Remove to serving dish.

*Serve with a basic marinara sauce or with the Easy Spaghetti.

Note: Internal temperature of the meatball should be 165°. If serving with sauce, figure 1/4 cup sauce per meatball. To serve as a hors d' oeuvre, make 3/4-inch size.

Reheating meatballs with or without sauce:
Microwave—4 minutes (6 minutes if frozen)
Oven—300° covered for 20 minutes
Stovetop—covered

EASY SPAGHETTI

INGREDIENTS

2 pounds Italian sausage, casings removed
2 1/2 pounds ground chuck
2 jars Classico Traditional Sweet Basil pasta sauce
2 tablespoons finely grated carrots
1 (28-ounce) can peeled tomatoes, crushed by hand, undrained (San Marzano recommended)
1 tablespoon dried oregano
1 tablespoon dried Italian seasoning
1 (24-ounce) jar petite diced tomatoes
1/2 cup water
1 pound thin spaghetti
1 teaspoon kosher salt

DIRECTIONS

1) In a large fry pan, brown Italian sausage.
2) Transfer to paper towel-lined plate and set aside.
3) In same fry pan, brown ground chuck.
4) Transfer to paper towel-lined plate; set aside.
5) Using either a 6-quart crock pot or saucepan, combine carrots, crushed tomatoes, oregano, Italian seasoning, diced tomatoes, and water.
6) Stir in Italian sausage and ground chuck thoroughly.

Yield: 10 to 12 servings

Crockpot—simmer on high for 2 to 3 hours
Saucepan—simmer on low heat for 2 to 3 hours

Bring 4 quarts of water to a boil. Add 1 tablespoon kosher salt and return to a boil. Add spaghetti and cook until al dente according to package directions.

Note: This can be prepared the day before up to the simmer point. Simply refrigerate and bring to a simmer the next day. Be sure to have lots of grated Parmigiano-Reggiano for serving. I like to serve with sliced sour pickles. The sourness of the pickle and the sweetness of the sauce create a melody on the taste buds.

In 2007, I represented Mississippi in the All-American Chicken Cooking Competition with this recipe. My first competition, as an adult, lit the fire in me for creating new dishes and competing more in the culinary world.

THAI CHICKEN LETTUCE WRAPS

INGREDIENTS

6 tablespoons water

1 stem lemongrass, peeled
  and smashed

(1 tablespoon finely minced fresh
  ginger and 1/3 cup fresh
  lemon juice may be substituted
  for the lemongrass)

1 pound ground chicken

4 tablespoons fish sauce

6 tablespoons fresh lime juice

1 teaspoon finely chopped
  Serrano pepper

4 tablespoons chopped fresh cilantro

4 tablespoons chopped fresh mint

1/2 lime

6 large iceberg lettuce leaves

1 red onion, cut in half
  and thinly sliced

1 medium red bell pepper, cut
  in half and thinly sliced

1 medium English cucumber, cut
  in half and thinly sliced

1/2 cup finely chopped dry
  roasted peanuts

1 package rice sticks, lightly
  fried (optional)

DIRECTIONS

1) In a fry pan, bring water and lemongrass to a boil over high heat; boil for 1 minute.
2) Remove lemon grass and add chicken; cook stirring for 4 minutes.
3) Stir in fish sauce, lime juice, Serrano pepper, cilantro, and mint.
4) Squeeze juice from 1/2 lime over chicken mixture.

5) Arrange lettuce leaves on a serving platter and spoon equal portions of the chicken mixture, onion, red bell pepper, cucumber, and rice sticks into each leaf.
  * Sprinkle peanuts on each, and top with plum sauce.

PLUM SAUCE

INGREDIENTS
1 cup plum jam
1/2 cup Thai sweet chili sauce

DIRECTIONS
1) Stir jam and chili sauce together.
   * Combine thoroughly.

Note: This is a great dish to set up as a make-it-yourself bar. Set out all ingredients and have each person make their own wrap.

Lemon grass is one of the most important flavorings in Thai cooking. Because it is very woody and tough, discard before serving.

**To keep lettuce leaves whole for wrapping, flip the head of lettuce upside down on your cutting board and cut out the core with a paring knife. Gently peel back the leaves from the thick bottom part and they won't tear.

It's hard to imagine civilization without onion.

—Julia Child

BASIC MARINARA

INGREDIENTS

1/4 cup extra-virgin olive oil
1 medium yellow onion, diced 1/4 inch
3 cloves garlic, minced
3 tablespoons chopped fresh thyme leaves
1/2 medium carrot, finely grated
1 (28-ounce) can crushed tomatoes in thick puree
1 (28-ounce) can peeled whole tomatoes, drained and crushed by hand
1 teaspoon kosher salt

DIRECTIONS

1) Heat olive oil in a saucepan over medium heat.
2) Add the onion and garlic and cook until light golden brown, about 8 to 10 minutes.
3) Stir in the thyme and carrot; cook for 5 minutes.
4) Add the tomatoes and bring to a boil, stirring often.
5) Reduce heat to low and simmer until sauce is thick, about 30 minutes.
6) Season with salt.

Yield: 4 1/2 to 5 cups

Note: Add 1/2 teaspoon crushed red pepper flakes for a spicy version.

Buying peeled shrimp is a little more expensive but makes this dish a lot easier to make. Roasting the shrimp instead of boiling gives the shrimp much more flavor.

ROASTED SHRIMP AND SHELLS

INGREDIENTS

1 1/2 pounds peeled shrimp

1 teaspoon kosher salt

1/2 pound small pasta shells

1 orange bell pepper, small diced

3/4 cup mayonnaise

Zest of 1 lemon

2 teaspoons kosher salt

3/4 cup minced fresh dill

1 teaspoon fresh ground black pepper

1 tablespoon extra-virgin olive oil

1/2 teaspoon fresh ground black pepper

3 cups fresh corn kernels

1 pint grape tomatoes, halved

1/2 cup sour cream

1/4 cup fresh lemon juice

1 teaspoon fresh ground black pepper

3 teaspoons kosher salt

*Preheat oven to 400°F.

DIRECTIONS

1) Pat shrimp dry with paper towels and place them on a sheet pan.
2) Drizzle with olive oil, sprinkle with the salt and pepper, and toss together.
3) Spread in one layer and roast, turning once while cooking, just until pink and firm and cooked through, about 6 to 8 minutes.
4) Cool pan for 3 minutes.
5) Chop shrimp in half and set aside.
6) Bring a large pot of water to a boil, and add 1 tablespoon kosher salt and a splash of olive oil.
7) Add the pasta shells and cook until al dente, about 8 to 10 minutes.
8) Add the corn to the pasta water and cook for another 2 minutes.
9) Drain the pasta and corn in a colander, and pour into a large mixing bowl.

10) Add the diced pepper, tomatoes, and shrimp, tossing gently to combine.

   * Allow to cool slightly.
11) In a small bowl, whisk the mayonnaise, sour cream, lemon juice, salt, and pepper together until smooth.
12) Pour over the pasta mixture and mix well to fully combine the ingredients.
13) Stir in the dill, salt, and pepper.
14) Cover with plastic wrap and chill up to 6 hours before serving to allow the flavors to develop.

   * Check seasonings and serve chilled or at room temperature.

Yield: 8 servings

Note: If the sauce is too thick after chilling, add a little lemon juice to thin it.

Inspiration for this dish came from Ina Garten.

An enjoyable eating experience is fresh, lump crabmeat—a heady indulgence, delicate and yet full of the flavor of the sea, whether in a crab-cake or a stuffed crab, or better yet a crab salad or crab tart, or any of the other infinite variations in which the succulent flesh lends itself.

CRAB AND MUSHROOM QUICHE

INGREDIENTS
1 single crust pie shell
3/4 cup fresh mushrooms, sliced
1 tablespoon unsalted butter
1 cup cream
3 large eggs
1/2 cup mayonnaise
1 tablespoon all-purpose flour
1 teaspoon kosher salt
1/2 teaspoon freshly ground black pepper
1/4 teaspoon dry mustard
1 bunch green onions, chopped
3 ounces package slivered almonds
1 1/2 cups Gruyere or Swiss cheese, finely chopped
8 ounces fresh jumbo lump crabmeat
1/8 teaspoon ground nutmeg

Preheat oven to 350°F.

DIRECTIONS
1) Using a fork, prick bottom of piecrust and bake for 5 minutes.
2) Melt butter in a small frying pan over medium heat.
3) Add mushrooms and sauté until tender; set aside.
4) Combine cream, eggs, and mayonnaise.

5) Add flour, salt, pepper, mustard, onion, almonds, and mushrooms and mix.
6) Fold in cheese and crabmeat.
7) Pour into piecrust and sprinkle with nutmeg.
8) Bake for 45 minutes. Top will get a medium to dark golden brown.
9) Let rest for 10 minutes before cutting.

Yield: 6 to 8 servings

Traditional fajitas are skirt steak marinated in lime juice and spices, grilled and wrapped in a warm tortilla with grilled onions and peppers. This version features lean chicken breasts and a colorful array of vegetables, including carrots for sweetness and crunch and mushrooms for "meaty" flavor and extra nutritional value. Quickly sautéed with herbs and spices, then finished with a squeeze of lime, they may not be traditional fajitas, but you won't mind!

CHICKEN AND VEGETABLE FAJITAS

INGREDIENTS

1 tablespoon ground chili powder
1 teaspoon ground cumin
1 teaspoon kosher salt
1/2 tablespoon freshly ground black pepper
1/2 teaspoon dried oregano
2 tablespoons canola oil
2 tablespoons freshly squeezed lime juice, about 1 1/2 limes
2 (6- to 7-ounce) boneless skinless chicken breasts cut into 1/4-inch wide strips
1 tablespoon canola oil
1 medium carrot, peeled and julienned
1 cup sliced shiitake mushroom cups, stems removed and discarded
2 cloves garlic, minced
1 medium yellow onion, peeled and julienned
1/2 medium red bell pepper, stemmed, seeded, and julienned.
1/2 medium yellow bell pepper, stemmed, seeded, and julienned.
1 jalapeno pepper, stemmed, seeded, and chopped.
1/4 cup chopped fresh cilantro
12 to 16 flour tortillas, warmed*
2 limes cut into wedges

DIRECTIONS

1) Combine the chili powder, cumin, salt, pepper, and oregano in a small bowl; set aside.
2) Place the 2 tablespoons of oil, the lime juice, and half of the spice mix in a large Ziploc bag; seal and shake to mix the ingredients evenly.
3) Open the bag and add the chicken, then reseal the bag and knead gently to coat the chicken evenly with the marinade. Set aside at room temperature for 15 minutes.
4) Heat a large sauté pan over medium-high heat.
5) Add the chicken and cook until it has lost its pink color.
6) Remove the chicken and set aside. The chicken will not be fully cooked, as it will be cooked further later.
7) Return the pan to the heat; add remaining 1 tablespoon of the oil, and heat through.
8) Add the carrots, mushrooms, garlic, onion, and peppers.
9) Cook until they just begin to soften, about 2 minutes.
10) Return the chicken to the pan and cook until the chicken is just cooked through, about 2 to 3 minutes more.
11) Remove from the heat and stir in the cilantro.
12) Spoon the fajita filling onto a warmed plate and present with a basket of warm tortillas and lime wedges.

*Serve with sour cream, salsa, and any additional accruements preferred!

Yield: 6 to 8 servings

Note:

*To warm the tortillas: For soft tortillas, wrap the stack of tortillas in aluminum foil, and place in 250°F oven while making the fajita filling.

If you prefer crisper tortillas, preheat a cast-iron pan or skillet over medium-high heat, and place the tortillas on the hot surface for about 20 seconds per side. Stack the warmed tortillas in a basket lined with a cloth napkin or an insulated tortilla keeper.

New Orleans food is as delicious as the less criminal forms of sin.
—Mark Twain

BARBEQUED SHRIMP

INGREDIENTS

1 1/2 tablespoons Creole seasoning (Konriko recommended)
3 teaspoons crackled black pepper
2 teaspoons freshly ground black pepper
1/4 teaspoon ground red pepper
2 pounds jumbo head-on shrimp
1 clove of garlic, minced
1/2 cup dry white wine
1/2 cup Worcestershire sauce
2 tablespoon fresh lemon juice
2 sticks cold, unsalted butter, cubed
2 lemons cut in quarters

Preheat oven to 350°F.

DIRECTIONS

1) Combine Creole seasoning and black and red peppers.
2) Place shrimp in a large roasting pan, and sprinkle evenly with dry spice mixture.
3) Combine garlic, wine, Worcestershire sauce, and lemon juice in a saucepan over moderate heat.
4) Stir in butter, a few cubes at a time, stirring constantly and adding more only when butter is melted.
5) Remove from heat and pour over shrimp.
6) Distribute lemon quarters in pan.

7) Bake for 5 minutes, or until shrimp turns pink and sauce is thoroughly heated.
   * Don't overcook the shrimp, or they'll be tough and hard to peel.

*Serve with lots of crusty French bread for dipping!
Yield: 8 servings

Simplicity is the ultimate sophistication.
—Leonardo Da Vinci

Note: The shrimp fat from the head and the flavor from the shells add to this New Orleans dish. Peeled and deveined shrimp can be used, but flavor and ritual will be sacrificed. Removing the heads with a pinch and sucking out the buttery sauce—what a joyous occasion!

In the south, barbeque means pork. There is simply nothing in this world or the next that tastes like pig kissed by fire and bathed in smoke.

On the Hatcher side of my family, we have a reunion on the Sunday closest to the Fourth of July that has taken place for over seventy years. My grandfather would pit-cook a whole pig and a goat. It was and still is a grand event; the huge beast split and spatchcocked on a large metal grate covered with tin. A roaring fire of hickory wood where the hot coals are shoveled around the outer edges of the pit during the night and into the next morning. A basting mop made out of a tree branch and a handful of rags, Granddaddy would patiently mop the succulent beast with a potent combination of vinegar, lemons, and peppers, letting heat and smoke slowly transform a hunk of pork into a moist, tender delicacy. After Granddaddy passed away, Daddy continued the tradition (in the photo). Daddy, a WWII POW, passed away on September 11, 2019. Now my brother, Larry, carries on this tradition, making sure the pulled pork is at the forefront of the family reunion.

On the Sideline

SIDE DISHES

As vegetables go, carrots tend to be sweet, especially the ones with the greens still attached. The acidity of the vinegar with an addition of sugar gives the dish depth and balance.

RASPBERRY CARROTS

INGREDIENTS

4 large carrots, peeled
3 ounces unsalted butter
2 tablespoons premium quality Raspberry Vinegar (Paul Corcellet recommended)
1/4 cup granulated sugar

DIRECTIONS

1) Cut the carrots diagonally in 1/2-inch thick slices.
    * Blanch the carrots for 3 to 4 minutes.
2) Melt 1 ounce butter in a large skillet over medium-low heat.
3) Add the blanched carrots and heat through.
4) Remove carrots using a slotted spoon; set aside.
5) Add the remaining 2 ounces butter to the skillet.
6) When melted, add the sugar and stir until thickened.
7) Add the raspberry vinegar and stir until fully incorporated.
8) Add the carrots back into the raspberry glaze.
9) Stir to distribute the glaze over the carrots and hold until ready to serve.
10) Before serving, pour off excess raspberry glaze and heat through.

Yield: 4 servings

MACARONI AND CHEESE

INGREDIENTS

6 slices white bread, crusts removed, torn into 1/4- to 1/2-inch pieces
2 tablespoons unsalted butter
4 cups whole milk
1 1/4 cups crème fraîche
6 tablespoons unsalted butter
1/2 cup all-purpose flour
3 cups grated Gruyere
2 cups grated extra-sharp Cheddar cheese
1 cup grated Parmigiano-Reggiano cheese
1/2 teaspoon freshly grated nutmeg
1 1/2 teaspoons kosher salt
1/2 teaspoon freshly ground black pepper or ground white pepper
1 pound elbow macaroni, Cavatappi or Rigatoni

Cook pasta according to package directions, 6 to 8 minutes, drain well.
Preheat oven to 375°F.
Butter a 3 to 4-quart casserole dish. Set aside.

DIRECTIONS

1) Place bread in a medium bowl.
2) In a small saucepan, melt the 2 tablespoons of butter over medium heat.
3) Toss melted butter and breadcrumbs; set aside.
4) Heat milk and crème fraiche over medium heat (do not boil).
5) In a large saucepan, melt the 6 tablespoons of butter over medium heat.
6) Reduce heat to low, whisk in flour, and cook, stirring for 2 minutes.
7) Slowly whisk in warm milk mixture until smooth.
8) Cook, whisking frequently, until thickened, about 10 to 14 minutes.
9) Remove from heat, stir in 2 cups Gruyere, 11 /2 cups cheddar, 1/4 cup Parmigiano-Reggiano, nutmeg, salt, and pepper.

10) Add the cooked pasta and mix until thoroughly combined.
11) Pour into prepared dish.
12) Sprinkle with remaining cheeses and breadcrumbs.
13) Bake until the cheese is bubbly and the top is golden, about 30 minutes.
14) Let stand 10 minutes before serving.

Yield: 10 servings

Sex is good, but not as good as fresh sweet corn.
—Garrison Keiller
Prairie Home Companion

CREAMED CORN

INGREDIENTS

6 ears fresh corn
2 tablespoons bacon grease
1 tablespoon unsalted butter
1 heaping tablespoon all-purpose flour
3/4 cup water
1/2 teaspoon freshly ground black pepper
1/2 teaspoon kosher salt

DIRECTIONS

1) Cut cobs in half and slice off tips of kernels.
   * Use the back of a knife and scrape what remains on the cob.
2) Heat bacon grease and butter in a large cast-iron skillet, over medium heat.
3) Add corn and stir in flour.
4) Add water, salt, and pepper; cook 5 minutes, stirring occasionally, until thickened.
5) Continue cooking, stirring occasionally until bottom gets a little crusty.
6) Continue to cook, scraping up crusty bottom from time to time, until creamy.
   * 30 to 40 minutes total.

Note: If using field corn, which is much starchier and less sweet, no added thickener is needed. Omit the flour.

The key to Southern creamed corn is not to cut off the kernels too close to the cobs. You want to slice off just the tips of the kernels, leaving a good bit on the cob. Then you can scrape what remains on the cob to extract its milky essence, filled with corn juices and pulp.

I like to use a Bundt pan, which helps to keep the kernels from flying all over the kitchen. Hold the cob in the hole of the pan, and the kernels will fall in the pan as you cut them off.

A couple of flitches of bacon are worth fifty thousand
Methodist sermons and religious tracts. They are great
softeners of temper and promoters of domestic harmony.
—William Cobbett

BAKED BEANS

INGREDIENTS

8 slices thick-cut bacon

1 1/2 cups chopped yellow onion

3 teaspoons minced garlic

3 (28-ounce) cans pork and beans, drained

1/2 cup dark brown sugar, packed

2 tablespoons Creole mustard

2 tablespoons Worcestershire sauce

1 tablespoon teriyaki sauce

1/2 teaspoon kosher salt

1/2 teaspoon fresh ground black pepper

DIRECTIONS

1) Cook bacon over medium heat until browned and crispy.
   * Crumble and set aside.
2) Reserve bacon drippings.
3) Cook onion and garlic in 2 tablespoons of the bacon drippings over medium heat, for 6 to 7 minutes, stirring frequently.
4) Preheat oven to 350°F.
5) Combine pork and beans remaining, reserved bacon drippings, onion mixture, brown sugar, mustard, Worcestershire sauce, teriyaki sauce, salt, and pepper.

6) Pour into a 15×10-inch casserole dish.
   * Top with crumbled bacon.
7) Bake 1 hour or until bubbly.

Yield: 12 to 15 servings

Note: No backyard barbecue is complete without baked beans and coleslaw.

MEDITERRANEAN COUSCOUS

INGREDIENTS

1 1/4 cups chicken broth
1 (5- to 6-ounce) package of toasted pine nut couscous
1/4 cup chopped fresh basil
4 ounces crumbled feta cheese
1 pint grape tomatoes, halved
1 1/2 tablespoons fresh lemon juice
1 teaspoon grated lemon rind
1/4 teaspoon freshly ground black pepper

DIRECTIONS

1) Heat broth and seasoning packet from couscous until it comes to a boil. This can be done in the microwave.
2) Place couscous in a large bowl.
3) Stir in broth mixture, cover with a plate. Let sit for 5 minutes.
4) Fluff couscous with a fork.
5) Stir in remaining ingredients.

*You can serve this warm, at room temperature, or cold!

Yield: 8 servings

Note: You can turn this dish into an entrée by adding 3 cups chopped, cooked chicken.

Light and fluffy couscous is a quick alternative to rice, pasta, or potatoes. It is made with semolina, the same ingredient as in pasta; couscous provides a good source of complex carbohydrates and B vitamins. Enjoy it by itself or with proteins, vegetables, and fruits.

Martha Washington's *Booke of Cookery* offers a recipe for pickling Green Asparagus. It instructs the reader to "hould ye roots in your hands and dip in ye green ends whilst ye water boyls. Soe doe by every bundle you have and when yrsparragus is cold, put it into a glass with verges and salt, and it will keep all ye year." Verges is an acidic sauce based on unripe grapes with lemon or sorrel juice; vinegar would be the modern equivalent.

PARMIGIANO-REGGIANO ASPARAGUS

INGREDIENTS

1 pound fresh asparagus
1/8 teaspoon kosher salt
3 tablespoons unsalted butter
1/8 teaspoon freshly ground black pepper
1/4 cup grated Parmigiano-Reggiano

DIRECTIONS

1) Butter a casserole dish large enough to accommodate asparagus with only a little overlapping.
2) Wash and trim asparagus.
3) Pour 1-inch of water into a large skillet over medium-high heat.
4) Add asparagus and salt; cook for 5 to 7 minutes. Or just until spears are just beginning to bend.
5) Remove from water and plunge into an ice bath to halt cooking.
6) Place asparagus in prepared casserole dish, slightly overlapping.
7) Dot with butter and sprinkle with the cheese and black pepper.
8) Bake until cheese melts, about 10 to 12 minutes.

HERB TOMATO TART

INGREDIENTS

Pastry for 9-inch pie dish
12 large ripe tomatoes, sliced 1/2-inch thick
1/3 cup Panko breadcrumbs
3/4 teaspoon finely chopped fresh basil
3 teaspoons finely chopped fresh Italian parsley leaves
1/4 teaspoon finely chopped fresh thyme leaves
1/8 teaspoon kosher salt
1/4 teaspoon freshly ground black pepper
1 tablespoon unsalted butter, melted
1 cup grated Parmigiano-Reggiano cheese

Preheat oven to 350°F.

DIRECTIONS

1) Arrange tomatoes in pastry crust.
2) Combine breadcrumbs, basil, parsley, thyme, salt, pepper, butter, and Parmigiano-Reggiano, and sprinkle evenly over tomatoes.
3) Bake for 30 minutes or until top is golden brown.

Yield: 6 servings

DEVILED EGGS

12 large eggs
6 tablespoons mayonnaise
1/4 cup sweet pickle relish
1 tablespoon country-style Dijon mustard
2 teaspoons dill pickle juice
1 1/2 teaspoons prepared mustard
1/4 teaspoon celery seed (*optional*)
1/4 teaspoon fresh ground black pepper
Garnish: paprika, crumbled bacon, chopped chives

DIRECTIONS

1) Place eggs in a large saucepan with enough cold water to cover by 2 inches.
   * Bring to a hard boil over high heat.
2) Remove from heat, cover, and let sit for 10 minutes.
3) Pour off hot water and run cold water over eggs to cool and stop cooking.
4) Shake the pan to crack the eggshells gently all over.
   * This releases the sulfur that can discolor the yolks.
5) Peel eggs under running water.
   Halve eggs lengthwise. Remove yolks and place in a small bowl.
6) Mash yolks with a fork until crumbly.
7) Add mayonnaise, pickle relish, country-style Dijon mustard, dill pickle juice, prepared mustard, celery seed (if using), and pepper to the yolks, mixing until well combined.
8) Spoon or pipe egg yolk mixture evenly into egg whites.
   * Garnish if desired.

Note: The perfect consistency for deviled eggs and egg salad is yolks that are soft and waxy rather than dry and crumbly.

CORNBREAD DRESSING

INGREDIENTS

1 hen

6 cups chicken broth

4 cups water

1 (10- to 12-inch) skillet of cooked cornbread

2 large onions, chopped

4 stalks celery, chopped

1 tablespoon unsalted butter

1 tablespoon extra-virgin olive oil

1 sleeve saltine crackers, crushed

2 tablespoons poultry seasoning

2 teaspoons rubbed sage

1 teaspoon kosher salt

1 teaspoon freshly ground black pepper

7 cups chicken broth

5 slices white bread, broken into small pieces

5 large eggs, beaten

DIRECTIONS

1) Remove gibbets from bird.
2) Wash gibbets and bird well (inside and out).
3) Cook hen and gibbets in chicken broth and water for 2 to 2 1/2 hours.
4) Skim fat from pot at end of cooking.
5) *Preheat oven to 350°F. Grease a large baking pan; set aside.*
6) In a large bowl, crumble cornbread.
7) Warm the butter and olive oil in a medium frying pan over medium heat.
8) Add onions and celery, cooking until onion is translucent, about 3 to 4 minutes. Pour over cornbread.
9) Add crushed crackers, poultry seasoning, sage, salt, and pepper, stirring gently to combine.
10) Pour 6 cups of the hot chicken broth over the cornbread mixture.

11) Scatter the bread picccs over the mixture and let sit for 5 to 6 minutes to absorb some of the broth.
12) Add the beaten eggs and thoroughly combine.
13) Mixture should be fairly juicy for a moist dressing.**
14) Pour into prepared pan and bake for 45 to 50 minutes.
  * Until cooked through and golden brown.

A three-year-old gave this reaction to her Christmas dinner:
"I don't like the turkey, but I like the bread he ate."
—Author Unknown

Note: In every Southern kitchen, the cornbread dressing will taste a little different. Some include pieces of turkey or chicken, more or less onion, more sage or no sage, and some prefer dry dressing rather than moist.

**If you are making giblet gravy, reserve 4 heaping tablespoons of dressing mixture.

Mother always said that your dressing will be as good as your cornbread.

GIBLET GRAVY

INGREDIENTS
Reserved dressing mixture
1 to 2 cups chicken broth
Hen giblets, chopped

DIRECTIONS
1) Combine dressing mixture.
2) 1 cup chicken broth and giblets in a saucepan over medium heat.
3) If mixture is too thick, add more broth (until desired consistency).
4) Simmer on low heat until ready to serve.

Note: A Southern favorite for roast turkey and always seen on the table at a Southern Thanksgiving or Christmas meal.

MYLES'S HOLIDAY STUFFING

INGREDIENTS
1 pound hot breakfast sausage
1/2 cup finely diced celery
3 sticks unsalted butter
1/2 teaspoon ground marjoram
1/2 teaspoon ground thyme
1 teaspoon garlic powder
3/4 teaspoon ground sage
1 package cornbread stuffing (Pepperidge Farms recommended)

Preheat oven to 350°F. Butter a 1 1/2- to 2-quart casserole dish.

DIRECTIONS
1) Cook sausage and celery over medium heat; drain well.
2) Add butter, cooking until melted.
3) Add marjoram, thyme, garlic powder, sage, and cornbread stuffing; stir until well combined.
4) Pour into greased casserole dish. Bake until heated through and top is browned.

Yield: 6 to 8 servings

Note: Myles Frank is a very dear friend that introduced me to Greg. It took him several months to convince me to go on my first and only blind date. After all, I am a Southern girl and Greg is a Yankee and an artist. I wasn't sure what to expect. Little did I know that this one chance meeting would turn into a lifetime commitment of love, support, and admiration. I thank you, Myles, for that night at the Fish Camp and for always being my friend. You are missed by everyone that knew and loved you.

Sweet potato casserole is a real Deep South dish and a tradition at the holiday table. This recipe is my version of taking the ordinary to extraordinary.

HOLIDAY SWEET POTATOES

INGREDIENTS

8 large sweet potatoes
1/2 cup unsalted butter, room temperature
1/2 cup light brown sugar, packed
1/2 cup all-purpose flour
1/4 teaspoon ground cinnamon
1/8 teaspoon ground nutmeg
1/4 teaspoon kosher salt
3/4 cup chopped toasted pecans
3/4 cup miniature marshmallows

Preheat oven to 400°F.

DIRECTIONS

1) Scrub sweet potatoes well under running water.
2) Prick sweet potatoes in a couple of places with a fork.
3) Put on an aluminum-lined jellyroll pan.
4) Bake for 45 minutes to 1 hour or until a knife inserted in the center goes in easily.
5) Mix butter, brown sugar, and flour until crumbly looking.
6) Add cinnamon, nutmeg, salt, pecans, and marshmallows; fold mixture together to combine.
7) Make a slit lengthwise down the center of each potato.
8) Push the ends together toward the middle until potato opens up.

9) Stuff the sweet potatoes generously with the sugar mixture.
10) Return to oven and bake until marshmallows are melted and the top is browned and bubbly, about 15 to 20 minutes.

Yield: 6 servings

Note: Mississippi produces 28 million pounds of sweet potatoes a year. Vardaman, Mississippi, is known as the "Sweet Potato Capital of Mississippi."

When I was growing up, I wanted these potatoes all the time. One of my mother's sisters, Aunt Shirley, lived with us while her husband was off fighting the war. She would make these for breakfast, and the house would smell so good. Aunt Shirley liked to cook onion with the potatoes, but I wasn't fond of the onion, so she left it out most of the time. My daughter, Hope, loves these as much as I do, and she will call and request that I make smothered potatoes.

SMOTHERED POTATOES

INGREDIENTS
3 tablespoons bacon grease
5 Idaho potatoes, thinly sliced
1/2 teaspoon kosher salt
1 small yellow onion, thinly sliced (optional)
3 slices bacon, diced (optional)
1/2 teaspoon freshly ground black pepper

DIRECTIONS
1) In a heavy bottom skillet with a cover, heat the bacon grease over medium heat.
2) Add the potatoes, bacon, and salt.
3) Cover the skillet and cook for 10 to 15 minutes.
4) Remove the cover and cook until the potatoes are golden brown and crunchy.
    * About 10 to 12 minutes

Note: If you wish to add onion, use 1 small sweet yellow onion, thinly sliced and cook with the potatoes and bacon.

BROILED TOMATOES

INGREDIENTS

1 sleeve round buttery crackers, finely crushed

5 ounces cheese of choice, finely grated or crumbled (Feta, blue cheese, Parmigiano-Reggiano, etc.)

6 slices bacon, cooked and crumbled

1/4 cup butter, melted

3 large fresh tomatoes cut in half lengthwise

1/4 teaspoon kosher salt

1/4 teaspoon freshly ground black pepper

Preheat broiler.

DIRECTIONS

1) Combine crackers, cheese, and bacon.
2) Stir in butter, mixing well.
3) Place tomato halves, cut side up, on an aluminum foil-lined baking sheet.
4) Sprinkle evenly with salt and pepper.
5) Divide cracker mixture evenly among tomatoes.
6) Broil 5 inches from heat for 6 to 8 minutes or until lightly browned.

You don't have to cook fancy or complicated masterpieces—just good food from fresh ingredients.

—Julia Child

In the south, a fish fry is a social event, an outdoor ritual centered on big cast-iron pots, set on portable butane burners. Bream and crappie, fried whole, head removed, makes them particularly sweet, delectable, and succulent are fish-fry musts. The flesh is easy to pull off the bone. Essential fixings at any Southern fish fry are hushpuppies, sliced onions, French fries, coleslaw, Tabasco, and iced sweet tea. This recipe was shared with me by a dear friend, Bruce Martin.

BRUCE'S SOUTHERN COLESLAW

INGREDIENTS
4 cups chopped green cabbage
1/2 teaspoon kosher salt
1/4 teaspoon freshly ground black pepper
3/4 teaspoon celery seed
1/3 cup + 2 tablespoons dill relish (Vlasic recommended)
1/3 to 1/2 cup mayonnaise (Hellman's recommended)

DIRECTIONS
1) Place cabbage in a large bowl.
2) Add salt, pepper, and celery seed; stir to distribute throughout.
3) Add relish and 1/3 cup mayonnaise; mix until thoroughly combined.
4) If mixture seems dry, add additional mayonnaise.
5) Taste and adjust seasoning as desired.
   * Cover and refrigerate for a minimum of 2 hours to allow the flavors to come together.

Yields: 4 servings

The oldest story about hushpuppies originates in the early 1700s in the settlement of Nouvell Orleans, later renamed New Orleans. They were created by a group of Ursuline nuns who came from France and converted cornmeal into a delicious food they named croquettes de maise. The popularity of these croquettes spread rapidly throughout the Southern states. Later, an African cook in Atlanta is said to have given the name "hushpuppy" while frying a batch of catfish and croquettes. Nearby a puppy began to howl, and to quiet the puppy, she gave it a plateful of croquettes and said, "Hush, puppy!" Since then the name was cut and has been used ever since.

JEAN'S HUSHPUPPIES

INGREDIENTS

2 1/2 cups self-rising white cornmeal
1/2 cup self-rising flour
1/2 medium yellow onion, finely diced
2–4 finely chopped fresh jalapeno
    peppers

1 cup buttermilk or beer
1 large egg, beaten slightly
Peanut oil for frying

DIRECTIONS

1) Pour oil to a depth of 2 inches in a Dutch oven and heat oil to 325°F.
2) Combine cornmeal, flour, onion, and jalapeno.
3) Add buttermilk and egg, stirring just until moistened.
4) Let mixture rest at room temperature for 15 minutes.
5) Using a cookie scoop, drop into hot oil.
6) Fry until golden brown, turning once, 2 to 3 minutes per side.
7) Drain on a wire rack with a paper towel-lined sheet pan underneath.
8) Sprinkle with salt immediately and serve.

Yield: 3 dozen

Make It Your Own

BUTTERS, CONDIMENTS, CREAMS, PESTOS, SAUCES

In the orchestra of a great kitchen, the sauce chef is a soloist.
—FERNAND POINT

Aunt Hattie was my granddaddy's sister who was married to my granny's brother. She lived on the Cahaba River and took me fishing with Granny. We would leave at dawn in the boat and be gone for most of the day. They gave me a bent straight pin for a hook. I would take out a worm and say, "You alive," and touch him; if he wiggled, I would say, "Yepp," and put him on my hook. I would drag that worm on the hook all the way back to the shore and never lost him, but I didn't catch any fish with that hook either. But I sure had fun.

AUNT HATTIE'S CHOW

INGREDIENTS

1 market basket of ripe but firm tomatoes
8 green bell peppers, finely chopped
7 yellow onions, finely chopped
Big handful of hot peppers, finely chopped
1 cup granulated sugar
1 quart white vinegar

1/2 cup kitchen salt
1 teaspoon celery powder or flakes
1 tablespoon ground ginger
1 tablespoon ground cinnamon
1 tablespoon ground allspice
1 tablespoon ground cloves
2 tablespoons dry mustard (Make a paste with water)

DIRECTIONS

1) Peel and quarter tomatoes.
2) Add bell pepper, onion, and hot pepper.
3) Add in sugar, vinegar, salt, celery powder, ginger, cinnamon, allspice, cloves, and mustard paste, stirring to combine.
   * Bring to a boil over medium heat for 3 hours or to desired consistency.
4) Pour into hot glass jars.
   * Seal and process in boiling water for 10 minutes.
5) Cool and store in the root cellar.

Note: A market basket of tomatoes is about 20 to 25 tomatoes and a big handful of hot pepper is about 6 to 8 small peppers.

BLUEBERRY BARBEQUE SAUCE

INGREDIENTS

6 cups fresh blueberries
2/3 cup honey
1/2 cup ketchup
1 jalapeno pepper, seeded and minced
1/2 cup finely chopped shallots
1 tablespoon grated fresh ginger
2 tablespoons fresh lime juice
1/2 teaspoon dry mustard

DIRECTIONS

1) Combine all ingredients in a saucepan.
   * Bring to a boil over medium heat.
2) Reduce heat and simmer 45 minutes or until thickened.

Note: Excellent served as a condiment to pork tenderloin or beef brisket.

PEPPER JELLY MARINADE

INGREDIENTS

1/2 cup pepper jelly
1/2 cup dry red wine
Zest and juice of 1 orange
2 tablespoons red wine vinegar
1 tablespoon chopped fresh rosemary
1 teaspoon red pepper flakes, crushed
1/2 teaspoon sea salt
1/4 teaspoon freshly ground black pepper

DIRECTIONS

1) Combine all ingredients.
2) Marinate protein at least 2 hours.
   * Preferably overnight

Note: Excellent with chicken or pork.

MANGO-PINEAPPLE SALSA

INGREDIENTS

2 ripe mangos, chopped
1 cup chopped fresh pineapple
1 large jalapeno, seeded and minced
1/4 cup minced red onion
1/4 cup chopped fresh cilantro
2 tablespoons fresh lemon juice

DIRECTIONS

1) Combine all ingredients and mix well
2) Serve at room temperature or chilled.

Yield: 1 1/2 cups

Note: Excellent served as a dip or as a condiment to pork or chicken. To reduce the strong flavor of onion in salsas and other raw dishes, chop the onion and rinse in cold water three times. Let them sit in the final rinse water for 30 minutes. Drain and dry. Onions will retain the crispness.

CAPER DILL SAUCE

INGREDIENTS

1 cup mayonnaise
2 tablespoons Dijon mustard
2 tablespoons small capers, drained and coarsely chopped
1 tablespoon fresh lemon juice
1 tablespoon chopped fresh dill

DIRECTIONS

1) Combine all ingredients until mixed thoroughly.
2) Chill until ready to serve.

Yield: 1 1/2 cups

Note: This is excellent served with salmon and beef tenderloin.

PECAN SAUCE

INGREDIENTS

6 tablespoons unsalted butter
1/2 cup toasted, chopped pecans
1/2 teaspoon lemon zest
3 tablespoons fresh lemon juice
1 teaspoon Worcestershire sauce
1/2 teaspoon kosher salt
2 tablespoons chopped fresh Italian parsley

DIRECTIONS

1) Toast the pecans either in the oven (350°F) or stovetop until fragrant.
2) For 6 to 8 minutes or on top of the stove over medium-high heat until fragrant.
3) Add lemon juice, lemon zest, Worcestershire, and salt to pecans.
4) Cook until heated through, about 2 to 3 minutes.
5) Stir in chopped parsley.

Yield: 6 servings

PECAN BOURBON CARAMEL SAUCE

INGREDIENTS

1 cup granulated sugar
3/4 cup heavy cream
3 tablespoons bourbon
1 teaspoon fresh lemon juice
1 cup chopped, toasted pecans

DIRECTIONS

1) Put sugar in a heavy saucepan.
2) Cook over moderately low heat, stirring with a fork to help sugar melt evenly.
3) Once sugar is melted and pale golden, stop stirring.
4) Continue to cook caramel, swirling pan until deep golden in color.
5) Remove from heat and carefully add cream, bourbon, lemon juice, and pecans.
   * Caramel will steam and harden.
6) Return to heat and simmer, stirring until caramel is dissolved, about 5 minutes.

Note: To toast pecans, put on cooking sheet and cook at 350°F for 3 to 5 minutes. Remove immediately from cookie sheet and place on paper towels.

PEANUT BUTTER SAUCE

INGREDIENTS
1/3 cup creamy peanut butter
1/4 cup confectioner's sugar
2 tablespoons milk

DIRECTIONS
1) Thoroughly mix peanut butter and confectioner's sugar together.
2) Add 1 tablespoon of milk and mix well.
3) Add the other tablespoon of milk and mix.

* If sauce is too thick, add a little more milk at a time, until desired consistency.

RASPBERRY SAUCE

INGREDIENTS

2 cups fresh raspberries
2 cups water
1/4 cup granulated sugar
2 tablespoons cornstarch
2 tablespoons water

DIRECTIONS

1) Combine raspberries, 2 cups water, and sugar in a saucepan; bring to a boil.
2) Reduce heat and simmer for 30 minutes.
3) Pour mixture through a wire-mesh strainer into a bowl and discard seeds.
4) Combine cornstarch and 2 tablespoons water, stirring until smooth.
5) Add cornstarch mixture to raspberry mixture.
6) Cook over medium heat, stirring constantly, until mixture comes to a boil.
    * Cook for 1 minute, stirring constantly.
7) Remove from heat and let cool.

Note: For a decorative plate, put some of the raspberry sauce in the center of the plate. Then dot the sauce with whipping cream. Carefully pull a toothpick through the middle of each dot.

*This is excellent served with Chocolate Pate and the Key Lime Pound Cake.

COMPOUND BUTTERS

Good butter is the most important ingredient in the kitchen. You must never use anything but butter, and it must always be the very, very best you can buy.

The Swedish say, "Food tastes better made with butter and love." Compound or flavored butters can make any meal seem like a special occasion, and yet they are so easy to make. The following recipes for quick and easy butters will delight family and friends.

STRAWBERRY BUTTER

INGREDIENTS

10-ounce package frozen sweetened strawberries, thawed
1 cup unsweetened, unsalted butter, room temperature
3/4 cup confectioners' sugar, sifted
1 1/2 teaspoons grated orange peel

DIRECTIONS

1) Combine all ingredients in food processor.
2) Blend until smooth, scraping bowl occasionally, about 5 minutes.
3) Transfer strawberry butter to medium bowl.
4) Cover and chill.

Note: Compound butters make excellent gifts. Cut butter into disks and package in attractive containers. Place butter-filled dish on a square of clear cellophane, pull up corners, tie with pretty ribbon, and you have an easy and low cost gift of friendship.

Tip: An excellent source for small, attractive, and affordable glass dishes is the local thrift store.

ORANGE BUTTER

INGREDIENTS

1/2 cup unsalted butter, softened
1/4 cup orange marmalade

DIRECTIONS

1) Stir together butter and marmalade until well blended.
2) Serve immediately, or cover and chill until ready to serve.
   * Refrigerate up to 1 week.

Yield: 3/4 cup

Note: You can make other fruit butters by substituting the orange marmalade for marmalade or preserves of choice.

*Serve with hot biscuits for breakfast or with hot bread or rolls for dinner.

LEMON-DILL BUTTER

INGREDIENTS

2 cups fresh lemon juice
3 tablespoons finely chopped fresh dill
1 cup unsalted butter, slightly softened
1/8 teaspoon kosher salt
1/8 teaspoon fresh ground black pepper

DIRECTIONS

1) Place lemon juice in a non-reactive saucepan.
   * Cook until reduced to 3 tablespoons forming lemon syrup.
2) Stir the butter, lemon syrup, dill, salt, and pepper until well blended.
3) Scrape into a small bowl or ramekin.
   * Chill for 1 hour before serving.

Sweet Endings

Stressed spelled backwards is Desserts. Coincidence? I think not!

—AUTHOR UNKNOWN

ORANGE COCONUT BALLS

INGREDIENTS

1 small box vanilla wafers
1/2 cup unsalted butter, melted
1 box powdered sugar
6-ounce can of frozen orange juice, thawed
1/2 cup finely chopped pecans
6 ounces sweetened flaked coconut

DIRECTIONS

1) Pulse vanilla wafers in food processor until fine crumbs.
2) Mix butter and sugar on low speed.
3) Add orange juice and pecans, mixing well.
4) Gradually add vanilla wafer crumbs, mixing until well combined.
5) Cover and chill for 1 hour.
6) Once chilled, roll into balls the size of golf balls.
7) Roll in flaked coconut and place in freezer.

Can be served frozen or at room temperature.

Lemon bars or squares are very popular in the South, especially for graduation parties, baby and wedding showers, and teas. Best-loved recipes are often those we inherit from family and friends. Passed along on bits and pieces of tattered paper and dog-eared recipe cards, they are treasures.

LEMON BARS

INGREDIENTS

Crust
1 cup unsalted butter, room temperature
1/2 cup confectioners' sugar
2 cups all-purpose flour
1/4 teaspoon kosher salt

Filling
4 extra-large eggs, room temperature
2 cups granulated sugar
1 tablespoon fresh lemon zest
3/4 cup freshly squeezed lemon juice
3/4 cup all-purpose flour

Preheat oven to 350°F.
Line a 13×9-inch baking pan with parchment paper, allowing 2 to 3 inches to extend over sides.

DIRECTIONS

Crust
1) Pulse butter, sugar, flour, and salt in a food processor until mixture is crumbly, about 5 to 6 times.
2) Press mixture into bottom of prepared pan.
3) Bake 15 to 20 minutes or until lightly browned; let cool on wire rack.

Filling

1) Beat eggs at medium speed until foamy.
2) Add sugar, lemon zest, lemon juice, and flour and beat on low until smooth.
3) Pour lemon mixture over baked crust.
4) Bake 25 to 30 minutes (or until filling is set).
5) Cool to room temperature on a wire rack.
6) Lift from pan onto wire rack, using parchment paper sides as handles; let cool completely.
7) Remove paper, cut into 2-inch squares, and sprinkle with confectioners' sugar.

Yield: 24 squares or 48 triangles

Lemon Bar Variations:

Add 1/2 cup ground toasted almonds and 1 teaspoon fresh lemon zest to the crust.

Add 1/2 cup finely chopped unsalted cashews to the crust.

Add 1/3 cup sweetened flaked coconut to the lemon mixture and garnish with toasted coconut.

Garnish with crushed lemon drops.

LIMONCELLO SORBET

INGREDIENTS

2 cups granulated sugar
2 cups water
1 tablespoon finely shredded lemon peel
1 1/2 cups fresh lemon juice
2 tablespoons Limoncello

DIRECTIONS

1) Mix sugar and water in a saucepan and bring to a boil, stirring until sugar dissolves.
2) Whisk in lemon peel, lemon juice, and Limoncello.
   * Cover and chill for 1 to 2 hours.
3) Pour into a 2-quart ice cream maker. Freeze according to manufacturer's instructions.
   * Pour into a container and put in freezer for 8 to 24 hours.

CHOCOLATE PÁTE

INGREDIENTS

2 pounds high quality milk chocolate (Callebaut)
12 ounces unsalted sweet cream butter
1/2 cup raspberry liqueur (Chambord)
1 cup water
4 egg yolks

DIRECTIONS

1) Combine chocolate, butter, liqueur, and water in top of double boiler until chocolate melts.
2) Whisk in egg yolks.
   * Strain into plastic-lined mold or pan of desired shape and chill.

To serve:
Slice pate and decorate plate with swirls of melted chocolate.
I like to serve this with a raspberry coulis and fresh raspberries.
This pairs well with a nice, full-bodied oak Cabernet Sauvignon.

RULES OF PERFECT PIE BAKING

1) Keep everything cold.
2) Don't add too much liquid.
3) Handle the dough as little as possible.
4) Refrigerate the dough.
5) Use young crusts for pecan pies and cream pies.
   * Place the freshly made pie dough in a pie pan, punch holes in the bottom of the crust, and freeze for at least 1 hour before baking.
   * There's no need to prebake the pie shell.
6) Use day-old crusts for fruit pies.
   * Make the dough the day before and leave on the counter overnight in a bowl covered loosely with a cloth.
   * This gives the crust a shine as it bakes.
7) Never use an egg wash on the crust.
   * Brushing a piecrust with egg wash before baking just makes the top of the pie brown before the bottom of the pie has time to cook through completely.
8) Bake pecan pie on the bottom rack.
   * This ensures the crust is perfectly baked through by the time the filling is set.
9) Start fruit pies on the top rack of the oven and then move them to the bottom rack.
   * Begin baking double-crust pies at 400°F. After 20 minutes, move them to the bottom rack and reduce the temperature to 350°F.
10) Let the pie cool completely, even overnight.
    * Give the pie time to set up, and you never have to worry about the filling running all over the plate.
11) King Arthur flour is unbleached and is best for basic pastry dough. It is milled from hard spring flour, has a higher protein level (12%), and strong gluten structure, which allows you to work in the fat needed for extra flakiness.

It takes a lot of dough to make the upper crust.
—Alfred E. Newman

BASIC PIECRUST

INGREDIENTS

3 cups all-purpose unbleached flour plus more for dusting
1 teaspoon kosher salt
1 teaspoon baking powder
8 tablespoon frozen shortening (Crisco) grated on large holes of a box grater
8 tablespoon frozen unsalted butter grated on large holes of a box grater
1/2 teaspoon distilled vinegar
1/2 to 2/3 cup ice water

DIRECTIONS

1) In bowl of stand mixer fitted with paddle attachment or in a large bowl using a hand mixer, combine flour, salt, and baking powder.
2) Add shortening and butter and beat on medium speed just until mixture resembles coarse meal, about 45 seconds.
3) Mix vinegar and 1/2 cup water in small bowl, and with mixer on low, mix in 1 tablespoon at a time until dough just comes together. Turn onto lightly floured surface and pat into 2 disks. Wrap in plastic wrap and refrigerate for at least 4 hours or up to 2 days or freeze for up to one month.
4) Liberally dust a work surface and your rolling pin with flour. Working quickly to keep the dough from warming up too much, roll out dough, rotating it a quarter turn every few rolls until it's about 1/4-inch thick. Roll the dough around the rolling pin and carefully unroll it into a deep 9-inch glass pie plate. Fold the overhanging dough under itself and press the dough to make it even. Crimp as desired.

PERSIMMON PIE

*Preheat oven to 425°F.

INGREDIENTS
1 (9-inch) piecrust
3 cups cooked and mashed persimmons
8 to 10 medium-size persimmons
3/4 cup granulated sugar
1/4 cup firmly packed light brown sugar
2 tablespoons all-purpose flour
3 large eggs, lightly beaten
1/2 teaspoon kosher salt
1/2 teaspoon ground ginger
1/2 teaspoon ground allspice
1 teaspoon ground nutmeg
1 teaspoon ground cinnamon
1/2 cup evaporated milk
1/2 teaspoon almond extract

DIRECTIONS
1) Cut off top of persimmons, scoop out pulp, and discard seeds.
2) Cook in small amount of water until fork tender; drain and mash until no lumps remain.
3) Mix granulated sugar, light brown sugar, all-purpose flour, kosher salt, and spices together; add to cooked and mashed persimmons.
4) Beat at low speed until combined.
5) Add eggs and beat until thoroughly combined.
6) Add evaporated milk and almond extract and stir until mixed.
7) Pour into prepared 9-inch pie pan lined with pie dough; bake at 425°F for 15 minutes.
8) Reduce heat to 350°F, and continue baking for an additional 40 to 45 minutes.

The persimmon is an exotic fruit with yellow-orange skin, which is at its sweetest when very ripe. To ripen firm fruit, place it in a paper bag at room temperature for 1 to 3 days. When ripe, store in refrigerator for up to 3 days.

HUG ME PIE

INGREDIENTS

1 (9-inch) deep-dish piecrust
1/2 cup all-purpose flour
1/2 cup light brown sugar, packed
6-ounce package Hershey hugs, cut in half
2 large eggs, room temperature
1/2 cup granulated sugar
1 cup butter, melted and cooled to room temperature
1 cup chopped toasted pecans

Preheat oven to 350°F.

DIRECTIONS

1) Beat eggs until foamy.
2) Add flour, sugar, and brown sugar; beat until well blended.
3) Stir in melted butter until combined.
4) Add hugs and pecans mixing until thoroughly combined.
5) Pour into a 9-inch deep dish pie shell and bake for 1 hour.

Note: You can make a pie shell or buy the pre-made in the refrigerated section of the grocery store. Pillsbury brand recommended.

TANGERINE ALMOND PIE

Preheat oven to 350°F.

Crust

INGREDIENTS

1 1/2 cups graham cracker crumbs	1/4 cup granulated sugar
1/2 cup finely chopped toasted almonds	6 tablespoons unsalted butter, melted

DIRECTIONS

1) Combine graham cracker crumbs, almonds, and granulated sugar.
   * Stir until well mixed.
2) Add melted butter, and stir until dry ingredients are thoroughly coated with the butter.
3) Press into the bottom and up the sides of a 9-inch pie pan.
   * Bake 10 to 15 minutes.

**Let cool while preparing filling.

Filling

INGREDIENTS

3 large egg yolks, room temperature	1 teaspoon tangerine zest
1 can of condensed milk	1/2 teaspoon orange liqueur
2/3 cup freshly squeezed tangerine juice	1/4 cup pureed tangerine

DIRECTIONS

1) Mix egg yolks and condensed milk.
2) Add tangerine juice, zest, orange liqueur, and tangerine pulp.
   * Stir gently to thoroughly combine.
3) Let stand at room temperature until thickened, about 15 minutes.
4) Pour into graham cracker crust and bake for 30 minutes.
5) Let cool completely on a wire rack.
   * Cover and chill for a minimum of 2 hours before serving.

Drenched with sweet glaze, this pound
cake sings with autumn flavors.
An apple is an excellent thing—until you have tried a peach.
—George du Maurier

FRESH PEACH CAKE

INGREDIENTS

1 cup unsalted butter, softened

3 cups granulated sugar

6 large eggs, room temperature

3 cups all-purpose flour

1/2 teaspoon kitchen salt

1 teaspoon baking soda

1/2 cup sour cream

3 cups peeled, chopped fresh peaches

3 teaspoons peach schnapps or peach nectar

1/2 teaspoon vanilla extract

**Preheat oven to 350°F.
Grease and flour Bundt pan.

DIRECTIONS

1) Cream butter and sugar until fluffy.
2) Add eggs one at a time, beating well after each addition.
3) Combine flour, salt, and baking soda, whisking to blend well.
4) Add dry ingredients alternately with sour cream to wet ingredients.
   * Beginning and ending with flour mixture.
5) Fold in peaches, peach schnapps, and vanilla.
6) Pour batter into prepared Bundt pan.
7) Bake 1 hour 15 minutes.
8) Cool in pan, on wire rack for 15 minutes.
9) Remove from pan and place on cake plate or stand.

Note: Adapted from a recipe given to me by my favorite Bullock cousin, Betty Seale.

Excellent served with a white chocolate ganache or a peach glaze!

Peach Glaze
3/4 cups confectioners' sugar
2 tablespoons peach schnapps
Combine until smooth.

White Chocolate Sauce
3 tablespoon heavy cream, heated
1 cup chopped white chocolate
Pour cream over chocolate, whisking until completely melted and smooth.

All you need is love. But a little chocolate
now and then doesn't hurt.

—Charles M. Schulzs

CONNOR'S BROWNIES

INGREDIENTS

3 tablespoons water
1 1/8 cups granulated sugar
1/2 cup unsalted butter
1 cup semi-sweet chocolate chunks
1/2 cup semi-sweet chocolate chips
3 large eggs, room temperature
1 1/2 teaspoon vanilla extract
1 1/8 cup all-purpose flour
3/8 teaspoon kitchen salt
1 1/2 cups semi-sweet chocolate chunks
3/4 cups chopped, toasted pecans

Preheat oven to 325°F.
Line 9×13-inch pan with parchment paper, overlapping edges by 2 inches; lightly grease parchment paper.

DIRECTIONS

1) Combine water, granulated sugar, and butter in a large saucepan.
2) Bring to a boil over medium heat, stirring constantly.
3) Remove from heat, and stir in 1 cup chocolate chunks and 1/2 cup chocolate chips until smooth; let cool for 5 minutes.
4) Add eggs, one at a time, stirring just until blended.
5) Stir in vanilla extract.
6) Combine flour and salt.

7) Stir in 1 1/2 cups chocolate chunks and pecans.

8) Stir flour mixture into chocolate mixture in saucepan until blended.

9) Spread onto a lightly greased, parchment paper-lined 9×13-inch pan.

10) Bake for 30 to 32 minutes.

11) Cool in pan on a wire rack; using parchment paper, take brownies out of pan and cut.

Yield: 24 brownies

My grandson loves to bake with me and has since he was three. One day, we were trying to decide what to make and thought peanut butter cookies would be good. Connor discovered the candy bars and suggested we put them in the cookies for a little surprise. What a hit these were! He still loves to cook; and I must say has turned into an excellent home chef.

CONNOR'S PEANUT BUTTER COOKIES

INGREDIENTS

1 3/4 cups all-purpose flour
1/2 cup granulated sugar
1/2 teaspoon baking soda
1/4 teaspoon kitchen salt
1/2 cup unsalted butter, room temperature
1/2 cup creamy peanut butter
1/4 cup honey
1 tablespoon whole milk
24 miniature chocolate-coated caramel-peanut-nougat bars

Preheat oven to 350°F.
Line a baking sheet with parchment paper.

DIRECTIONS

1) In a large mixing bowl, combine flour, sugar, baking soda, and salt.
2) Cut in butter and peanut butter.
   * Until mixture resembles coarse crumbs.
3) Beat in honey and milk until well combined.
4) Pat 1 tablespoon of the dough into a 2-inch circle.
5) Place 1 piece of candy in the center of the circle.
6) Shape the dough around candy to form a 1 1/2-inch ball.
   * Place on prepared pan.

7) Repeat with remaining dough and candy bars.
   * Bake for 12 to 15 minutes or until edges are lightly browned.
8) Cool on wire rack.

When baking, follow directions. When cooking, go by your own taste.

—Laiko Bahrs

KEY LIME POUND CAKE

INGREDIENTS

1/2 cup shortening

1 cup unsalted butter, softened

3 cups granulated sugar

6 large eggs, separated, room temperature

3 cups sifted cake flour

1/4 teaspoon baking soda

1/2 teaspoon baking powder

1/4 teaspoon kitchen salt

1 cup sour cream

2 tablespoons lime zest

1 teaspoon vanilla

1/2 cup fresh key lime juice

Preheat oven to 325°F.

Grease and flour a 10-inch (12-cup) tube pan; set aside.

DIRECTIONS

1) Beat shortening and butter at medium speed until creamy.
2) Gradually add sugar, beating until fluffy.
3) Add egg yolks, one at a time, beating well after each addition.
4) Sift flour, baking soda, baking powder, and salt together.
5) Gradually add flour mixture to butter mixture. Alternately with sour cream, beginning and ending with flour mixture, beating well after each addition.
6) Add lime zest and juice.

7) Beat egg whites at high speed until stiff peaks form; gently fold into batter.

8) Pour into prepared pan and bake 1 hour 30 minutes, or until cake tester inserted in middle comes out clean.

9) Cool in pan on wire rack for 10 minutes.

10) Remove from pan to wire rack.

KEY LIME GLAZE

INGREDIENTS

1 cup sifted confectioners' sugar
2 tablespoons fresh key lime juice
1/2 teaspoon pure vanilla extract

DIRECTIONS

1) Whisk all ingredients together until smooth.

Drizzle over cooled cake.

Note: In lieu of the glaze, serve individual slices with Raspberry Sauce[5].

---

[5] Raspberry Sauce pg. 176.

FRESH APPLE CAKE

INGREDIENTS

3 large eggs, room temperature
2 cups granulated sugar
1 1/2 cups canola oil
1 teaspoon vanilla extract
1 teaspoon ground nutmeg
1 teaspoon ground allspice
1 1/2 teaspoons ground cinnamon
3 cups all-purpose flour (White Lily recommended)
1 teaspoon baking soda
1 teaspoon kitchen salt
3 cups peeled, diced apples
1 cup chopped pecans

Preheat oven to 350°F.
Grease and flour a 10-cup tube or Bundt pan.

DIRECTIONS

1) Beat eggs slightly.
2) Beat in sugar, oil, vanilla, nutmeg, allspice, and cinnamon.
3) Sift flour, baking soda, and salt together.
4) With a large, wooden spoon, blend flour mixture into egg mixture.
5) Fold in apples and pecans.
6) Pour into prepared pan and bake for 1 1/2 hours.
   * Or until cake tester inserted in middle comes out clean.

ICING

INGREDIENTS

1/2 cup granulated sugar
1/2 cup light brown sugar
1/2 cup heavy cream
1/2 cup unsalted butter
1 teaspoon vanilla extract
1/4 cup dark rum
1/2 cup chopped toasted pecans

DIRECTIONS

1) Combine sugar, brown sugar, and heavy cream in a double boiler over medium heat.
   * Do not let boil.
2) Cook for 1 1/2 hours, stirring occasionally.
3) Add butter and cook additional 30 minutes.
4) Remove from heat; add rum, beating until smooth.
5) Let cool slightly; pour over cake. Sprinkle with toasted pecans.

Options: Cake can be made in an 11×17 rectangular pan.
Icing can be poured over individual servings.

Note: White Lily flour is best for cakes and biscuits. It is milled from soft winter wheat and was given much sifting, bleaching, and processing. Has relatively low protein content (8 or 9%) and has little gluten formation; therefore, produces light and flaky biscuits and tender cakes.

APPLE CRUMBLE

INGREDIENTS

5 Granny Smith apples, peeled, cored, and chopped
3 tablespoons all-purpose flour
1/2 cup light brown sugar
1 tablespoon fresh lemon juice
2 tablespoons pure maple syrup
1/4 cup finely chopped pecans

Crumble
1 cup all-purpose flour
1 cup granulated sugar
1/3 cup light brown sugar
3/4 teaspoon ground cinnamon
1/4 teaspoon kosher salt
8 tablespoons chilled unsalted butter, cut into pieces
1/4 cup coarsely chopped pecans

Preheat oven to 375°F.
Butter a 9×13-inch casserole dish. Set aside.

DIRECTIONS

1) Mix all of the filling ingredients together, tossing to coat all of the apples.
2) Pour into prepared dish.
3) In a food processor combine, flour, granulated sugar, brown sugar, cinnamon, and salt, pulsing to blend.
4) Add butter, pulsing until mixture forms pea-size lumps.
5) Add pecans and pulse 1 or 2 more times.
6) Sprinkle over filling and bake 40 to 50 minutes.
7) Cool on wire rack 10 minutes before serving.

Note: John Chapman, aka Johnny Appleseed, was actually distributing seeds as an investment in hard-cider stills. He was a bootlegger and sometimes a cross-dresser.

GARNISHING

Garnishes must be matched like a tie to a suit.

—Fernand Point

Presentation of food is almost as important as the food itself.

A finishing layer of flavors or textures—citrus zest, smoky bacon bits, a little sprinkling of flaky sea salt—all of that can transform a dish from ordinary to extraordinary.

CANDIED CITRUS SLICES

INGREDIENTS
1/4 cup water
3/4 cup granulated sugar
Thinly sliced citrus: lemons, limes, etc.

DIRECTIONS
1) In a large sauté pan, combine water and sugar; bring to a boil.
2) Add the citrus slices and simmer gently, uncovered, for 1 to 2 minutes or until just softened.
3) Transfer to a wire rack to cool.

GLAZED PECAN HALVES

INGREDIENTS

2 cups pecan halves
1/2 cup firmly packed light brown sugar
6 tablespoons dark corn syrup
Preheat oven to 350°F.

DIRECTIONS

1) Stir together all ingredients.
2) Spread mixture in a lightly greased aluminum foil-lined baking sheet.
3) Bake 12 to 15 minutes, stirring every 4 minutes.
4) Spread in a single layer on wax paper.
5) Cool completely, separating pecans as they cool or leave some in clusters.
6) Store at room temperature in an airtight container.

Yield: 2 cups

Note: These taste like the crunchy topping of a pecan pie. This simple recipe can transform even a store-bought dessert into a work of art. Add this garnish just before serving, as the glaze begins to melt whenever it touches a damp surface. It is also delicious in salad and stirred into softened ice cream.

CHOCOLATE LEAVES

INGREDIENTS

Several non-poisonous leaves, such as mint and basil leaves
1-ounce package semi-sweet chocolate

DIRECTIONS

1) Wash and dry non-poisonous leaves.
2) Melt chocolate over a double boiler.
3) Stir occasionally until the chocolate is smooth.
4) With a small spatula or brush, spread melted chocolate at least 1/16-inch thick on the back of each leaf. (Do not spread over leaf edges.)
5) Place chocolate side up on a plate, and refrigerate until firm.
6) Carefully peel each leaf from the hardened chocolate starting at stem end.
7) The side with the vein imprint is the right side; place right side up.

SUGARED FRUIT

INGREDIENTS

2 egg whites
2 teaspoons fresh lemon juice
Strawberries, grapes, blueberries, etc.
Caster sugar

DIRECTIONS

1) In a small bowl, whisk together egg whites and lemon juice; lightly brush on fruit.
2) Over additional small bowl, sprinkle brushed fruit with sugar.
3) Place on parchment paper to dry.
4) Store in refrigerator until ready to use; no longer than 1 week.

Note: Caster sugar is the same as superfine sugar. Sugared fruit is a versatile garnish that can be used for tops and sides of cakes, as embellishments for fruit tart, and as centerpieces for the table.

Techniques, Tidbits, and Tips

No one who cooks, cooks alone. Even at her most solitary, a cook in the kitchen is surrounded by generations of cooks past, the advice and menus of cooks present, the wisdom of cookbook writers.

—LAURIE CALWIN

KITCHEN MEASUREMENTS

Dash = Pinchless than 1/16 teaspoon

3 teaspoons = 1 tablespoon

2 tablespoons = 1/8 cup (1 fluid ounce)

4 tablespoons = 1/4 cup (2 fluid ounces)

5 1/3 tablespoons = 1/3 cup (5 tablespoons + 1 teaspoon)

8 tablespoons = 1/2 cup

12 tablespoons = 3/4 cup (6 fluid ounces)

16 tablespoons = 1 cup (8 fluid ounces)

3/8 cup = 1/4 cup + 2 tablespoons

5/8 cup = 1/2 cup + 2 tablespoons

7/8 cup = 3/4 cup +2 tablespoons

1 cup = 1/2 pint (8 fluid ounces)

2 cups = 1 pint (16 fluid ounces)

4 cups = 1 quart (32 fluid ounces)

2 pints = 1 quart

4 quarts (liquid) = 1 gallon

8 quarts (dry) = 1 peck

4 pecks = 1 bushel

16 ounces (dry) = 1 pound

MEASURE FOR MEASURE

Ingredient Equivalents

Chocolate
12-ounce package chocolate chips = 2 cups

Crumbs
1 cup soft bread crumbs = 2 slices bread
1 cup dry bread crumbs = 4 slices bread
1 cup graham cracker crumbs = 14 squares
1 cup finely crushed vanilla wafer crumbs = 22 wafers
1 cup chocolate wafer crumbs = 19 wafers
1 cup finely crushed gingersnap crumbs = 15 cookies

Dairy
6 tablespoons cream cheese = 3 ounces
1 cup cream cheese = 8 ounces
1 cup crumbled blue cheese = 4 ounces
1 1/4 cup grated cheese = 4 ounces hard cheese *(Parmesan and Romano)*

Cheddar and Swiss
1 cup shredded cheese = 4 ounces hard cheese

American and Monterey Jack
1 1/2 cups shredded cheese = 4 ounces soft cheese
2 cups whipped cream = 1 cup heavy cream
1 cup cottage cheese, sour cream, yogurt = 8 ounces

Fruit
1 cup sliced apple = 1 large
1 1/2 cups mashed or 2 cups sliced bananas = 3 medium

2 tablespoons fresh lemon or lime juice = 1 medium
1 teaspoon grated lemon or lime zest = 1 medium
4 teaspoon grated orange rind = 1 medium
1 cup fresh orange juice = 3 medium
6 cups sliced peaches = 8 medium
2 cups berries = 1 pint
4 cups berries = 1 quart
1 cup chopped tomato = 1 large
1 cup canned, diced tomatoes = 14 1/2-ounce can, drained

Nuts
3 cups chopped almonds = 1 pound shelled
4 cups chopped pecans = 1 pound shelled
4 cups chopped walnuts = 1 pound shelled

Pasta, Rice
8 ounces dry elbow macaroni = 4 cups cooked
8 ounces fettuccini = 3 3/4 cups
8 ounces angel hair = 5 1/2 cups
8 ounces spaghetti = 4 cups cooked
1 cup white rice = 3 cups cooked
1 cup converted = 4-cups cooked
1 cup instant = 1 1/2 cups cooked
1 cup brown = 3 to 4 cups cooked

Miscellaneous
1/2 cup crumbled bacon = 8 slices
1 large boned whole chicken breast = 2 cups cooked
1 tablespoon chopped herbs = 1 teaspoon dried herbs
1 clove garlic = 1 teaspoon chopped
1 pound raw shrimp in shell = 1/2 pound cooked shrimp
Shelled and deveined

ONE-POUND EQUIVALENTS

2 cups butter (4 sticks)
4 cups all-purpose flour
2 cups granulated sugar
4 1/2 cups powdered sugar
2 1/4 cups brown sugar, packed

Vegetables
3 cups chopped asparagus
4 cups chopped beans (string/green)
12 cups chopped broccoli
4 1/2 cups shredded cabbage (1 small)
1 cup sliced or grated carrots (1 large)
1 cup chopped or diced celery (2 medium celery stalks)
4 cups sliced cucumbers (2 medium)
4 cups chopped eggplant (6 cups cubed = 3 cups cooked)
4 cups chopped leeks (2 cups cooked)
5 to 6 cups sliced raw mushrooms (2 cups cubed) 1 1/2 pounds
1/2 cup chopped onions (1 medium raw)
1 cup shelled or dried peas or beans—2 1/2 cups cooked
1 cup diced bell pepper (1 large pepper)

IN A PINCH? SUBSTITUTE

Needed Ingredient Baking Product	Substitute
2 cups baking mix	1 3/4 cup all-purpose flour 2 1/2 teaspoon baking powder 3/4 teaspoon salt 1/3 cup shortening
1 teaspoon baking powder	1/2 teaspoon cream of tartar plus 1/4 teaspoon baking soda
1 cup cake flour, sifted	1 cup minus 2 tablespoons all-purpose flour
1 cup self-rising flour	1 cup all-purpose flour 1 teaspoon baking powder 1/2 teaspoon salt
1 tablespoon cornstarch (thickening)	2 tablespoons all-purpose flour
1/2 teaspoon cream of tartar	1 1/2 teaspoons fresh lemon juice or vinegar
1 cup powdered sugar	1 cup sugar plus 1 tablespoon corn starch (processed in food processor)
1 cup sugar, granulated	1 cup packed brown sugar or 2 cups sifted confectioners'
1 cup brown sugar, packed	1 cup sugar plus 2 tablespoons molasses
1 cup honey	1 1/4 cup sugar 1/4 cup water
1 cup molasses	1 cup honey or 3/4 cup sugar
1 whole vanilla bean	2 teaspoons vanilla extract
1 cup chopped pecans	1 cup regular oats, toasted
1 ounce unsweetened chocolate	3 tablespoons cocoa plus 1 tablespoon butter

1 ounce semi-sweet chocolate	1/2 ounce unsweetened chocolate 1 tablespoon sugar or 3 tablespoons semisweet chocolate pieces
6 ounce package semi-sweet chips, melted	2 ounces unsweetened chocolate 2 tablespoons shortening plus 1/2 cup sugar
4 ounces sweet baking chocolate	1/4 cup cocoa plus 1/3 cup sugar and 3 tablespoons shortening
1 cup light corn syrup	1 cup granulated sugar plus 1/4 cup water
Dairy	
1 cup buttermilk	1 tablespoon vinegar or lemon juice plus milk to equal 1 cup, or 1 cup plain yogurt
1 cup light cream	1 1/2 tablespoon butter plus whole milk to equal 1 cup
1 cup heavy cream, whipping	1/3 cup melted butter plus whole milk to equal 1 cup (for baking or cooking only; will not whip)
1 cup sour cream	1 cup plain yogurt plus 3 tablespoons melted butter or 1 cup plain milk plus 1 tablespoon corn starch
1 cup whole milk	1/2 cup evaporated milk plus 1/2 cup water
1 whole egg	2 egg yolks or 2 egg whites (do not substitute when making dough)
Vegetables	
1 pound fresh mushrooms	12 ounce canned mushrooms, drained
1 small onion, chopped	1 tablespoon instant minced onion or 1 teaspoon onion powder
3 tablespoons chopped sweet red pepper	2 tablespoons chopped pimento

3 tablespoons chopped shallots	2 tablespoons chopped onion plus 1 tablespoon chopped garlic
Seasonings	
1 clove garlic	1/8 teaspoon garlic powder or minced dried garlic
1 tablespoon chopped chives	1 tablespoon chopped green onion tops
1 tablespoon grated fresh ginger root	1/8 teaspoon ground ginger
1 tablespoon grated fresh horseradish	2 tablespoons prepared horseradish
1 tablespoon dried orange peel	1 1/2 teaspoon orange extract or 1 tablespoon orange rind
1 tablespoon candied ginger	1/8 teaspoon ground ginger
1 teaspoon garlic salt	1/8 teaspoon garlic powder plus 7/8 teaspoon salt
1 teaspoon ground allspice	1/2 teaspoon ground cinnamon plus 1/2 teaspoon ground cloves
1 teaspoon apple pie spice	1/2 teaspoon ground cinnamon 1/4 teaspoon ground nutmeg 1/8 teaspoon ground cardamom
1 teaspoon pumpkin pie spice	1/2 teaspoon ground cinnamon 1/4 teaspoon ground ginger 1/8 teaspoon ground allspice 1/8 teaspoon ground nutmeg
1 teaspoon dry mustard	1 tablespoon prepared mustard
1 tablespoon fresh herbs	1 teaspoon dried herbs or 1/4 teaspoon ground herbs
Miscellaneous	
1/2 cup balsamic vinegar	1/2 cup red wine vinegar (slight flavor difference)
1 cup tomato juice	1/2 cup tomato sauce plus 1/2 cup water

1 cup tomato sauce	1 (3-ounce) can tomato paste plus 1/2 cup water or 3/8 cup tomato paste plus 1/2 cup water
2 cups fresh, chopped tomatoes	1 (16-ounce) can (may need to drain)
1 (7-ounce) jar marshmallow cream	1 (16-ounce) package of Marshmallows, melted, plus 3 1/2 tablespoons light corn syrup
Alcohol	
1 tablespoon brandy	1/4 teaspoon brandy extract plus 1 tablespoon water
1/4 cup Marsala wine	1/4 cup white grape juice or 1/4 cup dry white wine plus 1 teaspoon brandy
2 tablespoons Amaretto	1/4 to 1/2 teaspoon almond extract
2 tablespoons bourbon or sherry	1 to 2 teaspoon vanilla extract
2 tablespoons brandy or rum	1/2 to 1 teaspoon bandy or rum extract
2 tablespoon Grand Marnier or other orange liqueur	2 tablespoons unsweetened orange juice concentrate or 2 tablespoons orange juice plus 1/2 teaspoon orange extract
2 tablespoons Kahlua or other coffee liqueur	1/2 to 1 teaspoon chocolate extract plus 1/2 to 1 teaspoon instant coffee diluted in 2 tablespoons water
white wine	equal measure white grape juice or non-alcoholic white wine
red wine	equal measure red grape juice or cranberry juice

PAN SIZES AND VOLUME

8×1 1/2-inch round = 4 cups
8 × 2-inch round = 6 cups
9 × 1 1/2-inch round = 6 cups
9 × 2-inch round = 8 cups
8 × 8 × 1 1/2-inch square = 6 cups
8 × 8 × 2-inch square = 8 cups
9 × 9 × 1 1/2-inch square = 8 cups
9 × 9 × 2-inch square = 10 cups
11 × 7 × 2-inch rectangle = 6 cups
15 × 10 × 1-inch rectangle = 10 cups
13 × 9 × 2-inch rectangle = 14 cups
8 × 3-inch spring form = 11 cups
9 × 2 1/2-inch spring form = 10 cups
9 × 3-inch spring form = 12 cups
10 × 21/2-inch spring form = 12 cups
8 × 4 × 2 1/2-inch loaf = 4 cups
9 × 5 × 3-inch loaf = 8 cups
1 3/4 × 3/4-inch mini-muffin cup = 2 tablespoons
23 /4 × 1 1/2-inch mini-muffin cup = 1/2 cup
10-inch fluted tube = 12 cups
10-inch tube = 16 cups

METRIC

1 teaspoon = 5 milliliters (4.9)
1 tablespoon = 15 milliliters (14.8)
1 cup = 240 milliliters (236.6)
1 gram = 0.035 ounces
1 ounce = 28 grams (28.35)
1 pound = 454 grams
1 liter = 1.06 quarts or 1,000 milliliters

BAKING TIPS

1) Sifting flour adds air for a lighter cake.
2) Sift dry ingredients with flour so they are blended in equality.
3) Hard brown sugar: place a wedge of apple in it and leave until softened.
4) Preheat your cookie sheet, muffin tins, or cake pans, you will get better results.
5) When softening butter, don't try to rush the process by popping the butter in the microwave. No matter how well you time it, the butter will begin to melt and lose some of its ability to hold air. Letting the butter and eggs sit at room temperature for 30 minutes to 1 hour will guarantee a better cake, brownie, cookie, etc.

COOKING TIPS

1) Plum or Roma tomatoes contain less water than other tomatoes, making them ideal for roasting.

2) Spray a grater with cooking spray before grating cheese, as this will prevent it from sticking to the grater.

3) Heat a knife in hot water and dry it off quickly before slicing fresh bread. This makes the job much easier.

4) Fresh lemon juice and salt will remove onion scent from hands.

5) Chewing a coffee bean will mask garlic breath.

6) To chiffonade is to cut leafy vegetables or herbs into ribbons. Stack some leaves and roll them into a cylinder before slicing them thinly.

7) For maximum flavor from dried herbs, rub them between the palms of your hands or crush them with your fingers.

8) To refresh stale chips and crackers: spread in a single layer on baking sheet. Heat them in an oven at 350°F for 5 minutes. Cool (they will crisp as they cool). Serve immediately or store in an airtight container up to 1 week.

9) Use fresh herbs singly in dishes to preserve their clear, fresh flavors and not overwhelm the profile of the other ingredients.

10) Fill ice cube trays with assorted leftover herbs and top off with water or vegetable broth. When frozen, remove herb cubes and place in Ziploc storage bag. Use as needed for a fresh herbal flare (soups, sauces, etc.).

11) Cilantro, parsley, mint, and basil should be stored in a tall glass with about 1 inch of water, cut ends down. Cover tops loosely with plastic wrap to allow the herbs to breath. Sage, thyme, and rosemary should be placed in a perforated bag or wrapped in plastic wrap and stored in the refrigerator's crisper.

12) Easiest way to slice goat cheese is with dental floss.

13) Add a pinch of kosher salt to fresh spices when using a mortar and pestle to keep seeds, pods from jumping; they are quickly reduced to powder by the sharp edges of the salt. Also works great with garlic and citrus zest.

14) Add a paper towel to the basket of a salad spinner with the greens. The towel efficiently absorbs excess moisture, making it easy to spin until dry.
15) Salt intensifies sweetness.
16) Squeeze a piece of onion through a garlic press to grate a small amount of onion easily.

ONE-MINUTE LESSON IN FOUR-STAR COOKING

Start with high heat—Searing imparts taste in everything from mushrooms to meat. Turn the flame way up, and let the food sizzle for a minute.

Shallots instead of onions—In any simple sautéed dish, try substituting shallots for onions. They are sweeter with less of a bite.

Perfectly dressed salad—Delicate greens need something light, like lemon and olive oil. Heavier lettuce, like romaine, wants heavier dressing, with a balsamic or mayonnaise base. Always pour dressing into the bowl first, then throw in greens and toss gently. It keeps leaves from being weighed down

Ditch the iodized salt—Use kosher salt for cooking (it's milder and sticks well to food) and sea salt for finishing (delicate and tasty).

Blanch for color and flavor—Restaurants' carrots are more orange and beans are greener because they're boiled for a minute in salted water, then thrown in an ice bath (which halts the cooking process).

SALT

Salt is the most critical ingredient in cooking, and learning to use it well is one of the biggest steps you can take in perfecting your cooking skills. Salt brings out all the flavors and makes food come alive. The impact that salt has is evidenced throughout your cooking, from savory to sweet.

Different ways and times to salt your food, each producing a specific result is crucial to building flavor. Salt as you go; seasoning onions, celery, and other ingredients as they are sweating brings out their full flavor and sweetness, resulting in a better finish.

With meats and poultry, salt anywhere between 8 and 24 hours, removing from the refrigerator 20 to 60 minutes prior to cooking. This is the time to add additional seasonings—herbs or spices—as the salt helps the flavor penetrate the muscle.

Salt seafood right before putting it into the heat. Pre-salting tends to firm up the seafood, affecting the texture.

Salting vegetables to be grilled or sautéed about 30 minutes in advance will pull out any additional liquid or bitterness. This will bring out all their sweetness and flavor.

Use kosher salt for seasoning and sea salt for finishing. Avoid iodized table or kitchen salt, which has an acrid chemical flavor.

BALANCE

The most important quality in a dish is balance. Once you have seasoned everything properly, you must make sure the flavors and textures are balanced.

Balance a rich central item with acidic and bitter component and a lean central item with fat (butter, cream, or bacon) and an acidic component.

Without a doubt, two of the most critical elements of a dish are fat and acid. The fat is what gives you that great mouth feel and helps satisfy your soul; it's the richness that makes food fulfilling.

The acidity cuts through the fat as you're eating while keeping your palate alive and jumping. Ways to add acidity—splash some vinegar into a braising liquid, add citrus to a butter sauce, or top a steak with pickled vegetables. Acidity helps to open up your palate and accept the flavors.

Varying textures are critical to the success of a balanced dish. Always consider the texture in a dish and make sure you have contrasts.

Final qualities of a dishes' competition are spicy and bitter. Bitter can create a great counterpoint to richness. Spice can be tricky, but when used correctly, it can help create great contrasts and flavors and really make food come alive. Remember that heat varies from chili to chili, so tasting is crucial.

Also, remember that most of the heat is in the ribs and seeds, which can be removed to temper the heat.

ACKNOWLEDGMENTS

Words cannot express my gratitude and love to my best friend and companion who has always believed in me—Greg Cartmell. He helped me organize my thoughts and get them down on paper. When I felt discouraged and wanted to give up, he lifted my spirits and assured me everything would eventually come together—that *Beyond Southern* would be completed in due time.

I want to thank my family for always believing in me and giving me their love and support. You are my roots and my foundation.

So many wonderful people have encouraged me to follow my dreams, to cook with passion, and to share my passion with others. To you, I am grateful.

I have an amazing close circle of friends that have supported, encouraged, advised, and loved me through good times and not so good times and who have been wonderful taste testers. I love each of you and am so fortunate to have you in my life.

INDEX

ABOUT THE AUTHOR

Born in Birmingham, Alabama, Debbie Martin is a true Southerner and a coal miner's daughter. She grew up in a small community outside of Bessemer called Hopewell until her early teens when her family moved to Mississippi.

Watching her grandmother cook gave her an affection for down-home Southern cooking. She entered and won her first cooking competition at the age of twelve, was chosen to represent Mississippi in the National Chicken Cooking Competition, and appeared on Food Network's *Ultimate Recipe Showdown: Hometown Favorites* where she came in second, losing by only one point.

Besides cooking, she has an affection for painting insects in watercolor.

Her inspiration for writing *Beyond Southern* came from a desire to share family traditions and recipes and with the hope that you will recreate them in your own home for a little taste of what life is like down South.

CPSIA information can be obtained
at www.ICGtesting.com
Printed in the USA
LVHW072109090323
741288LV00010B/588